M000228899

Will You Wipe My Tears?

By Joyce Jamerson

Spiritual "equipment" for the contest of life.

SPIRITBUILDING PUBLISHING
15591 N. State Rd. 9, Summitville, Indiana, 46070
SpiritBuilding.com

© SPIRITBUILDING, 2008, All Rights Reserved. No part of this book may be reproduced in any form without the written permission of the publisher. Printed in the United States of America.

Table of Contents

Dedicated to all those who want to help others

**In Memory of our
daughter, Jill
April 7, 1974 ~
September 18, 1993**

Some people come into our lives and quickly go.
Others stay for a while and move our souls to dance.
They awaken us to understanding with the passing
whisper of their wisdom. Some people make the sky
more beautiful to gaze upon. They stay in our lives
for awhile, leaving footprints on our hearts and we
are never, ever the same.

Flavia Weedn

FORWARD

My journey of grief has led to invitations to speak in various places, and eventually to speak at the Florida College Lectures in February of 2000. When the invitations to speak were first offered, it was a difficult decision. I didn't know if it would be a good thing; would it cause me to dwell more on grieving or take me to a place where I didn't need to be? Would I be happy doing it? But on the other hand, would I be happy *not* doing it? My decision was made easier because I could see a definite need for better understanding concerning grieving.

In addition, I couldn't picture myself standing before my Lord at judgment, knowing I had this information, to tell Him I didn't want to do His work.

Since the death of our daughter, clippings, poems and general information about grief have gone into a file drawer. You know how preaching families are about these things, I might need that sometime! So the file has served me well, although there were days when the memories were too vivid to continue, and the project had to be set aside. Rarely do we go out of town without someone mentioning *Helping the Grieving,* the tape that was made of the F.C. speech and how the tape of that speech has been copied and shared. This book has come about because of conversations with those who are grieving and comments from those who truly want to help but don't know where to start. The effort to get my thoughts on paper has been a true labor. Many times I wondered *what came over me; why in the world did I ever think I could write a book!*

Since I am neither a writer nor a public speaker, this venture has been blessed by God. We've done it together; I'm unable to do this alone. This shy servant has stood before hundreds, with shaking knees and an occasional tear, being convinced the message is needed. These pages are written to

Christians. We, of all people, should be able to comfort one another throughout the grieving process; however, if the grief of those around us lasts more than a few weeks, our sympathy bank seems to become overdrawn.

> **If the grief of those around us lasts more than a few weeks, our sympathy bank seems to become overdrawn**

So I hope you, the reader, can overlook the fact that I've been out of school for many years, and have long forgotten some of the elements of writing. Just accept my words as a small attempt to bring about better understanding, and through this understanding, to ease the pain of a friend. This work only briefly discusses many important topics, so it is my hope that it will inspire the need for deeper study.

There are several people to thank, especially those who proof read and gave me their constructive comments; but throughout this book, I have purposely not revealed many names. They know who they are and I am deeply grateful for each contribution. Many people helped my family throughout our grief journey and continue to do so. Hopefully, our focus is not on who did what, but on how to help others and how we can glorify God by doing so.

Scripture quotations are from the New American Standard Version of the Bible unless otherwise noted.

Will You Wipe My Tears?
A guide for helping the grieving

Introduction

My husband has often teased me about liking puzzles. He can't understand why anyone would cut a perfectly good picture into 1500 pieces! Many times, my daughter Jill and I would spread a puzzle out on the dining room table, and take days and even weeks to put it together. Sometimes the puzzle would just call our name, and anytime we passed by the table, we'd have to stop and find a few pieces. The reward comes when you see that lovely picture completed. There's a feeling of meeting the challenge and enjoying the accomplishment (although the space it took on my dining room table did become a problem!)

Once in a while someone will ask if I have a hobby. My usual reply is that *I like to cut up fabric and sew it back together again.* Now and then there's a puzzled look until they realize I'm talking about quilting! It's the same concept as a puzzle, but with a much broader sense of accomplishment. When you see it to completion, you have something that doesn't get torn up and put back into a box but involves the same principle of finding and putting together pieces. Cutting up fabric and sewing it back together may seem futile to some, but there are great rewards when you see the design come together.

Many other puzzles can come about in our lives. When our daily routines are disrupted by the bumps of life ~ illness, accidents, death ~ it may take a while to find all the pieces and get them in order again. The process of grieving is a large difficult puzzle with many pieces and it takes a long time to get the pieces in their proper place. Some struggle with this puzzle for a lifetime and, for some, a few pieces are always missing. Some work on their puzzle privately, refusing to speak of it; so we fail to learn from the experience of others and the cycle of

4

misunderstanding continues.

Most of us will face this puzzle at some point in life. For many, it's the death of a parent, spouse, or close friend. The puzzle becomes more difficult when we have to bury a child as children are our hope; our link to the future.

During the September 11 ceremonies in 2004, at the World Trade Center site, this statement was made:

Men who have lost their wives are called widowers. Women who lose their husbands are called widows. Children who have no parents are orphans but parents who have lost children ~ what are they called? There are no words to describe them.

Whether it is a sudden traumatic event or a long lingering illness doesn't seem to change the complexity of the puzzle. Birthdays, anniversaries, and special occasions will delay the process of putting the pieces in order and as we struggle with this, many do not understand. For others, it's just a day. For grievers, it's a memory.

The suddenness of a situation may bring many questions; questions about death, about God, and the ever puzzling, *why?* For the friends who gather around, the questions are: *What can we do? How can we help? What should we say?* Can we, will we wipe their tears?

How will you help?

Obviously, the needs of the moment will depend on the situation. At the onset, food, lodging, errands and babysitting may all be needed and we are happy to either fulfill the need or find someone who can. But beyond the obvious lies another set of questions.

How would you help a friend remember a special day? What is appropriate? What would be too much to say and what would be too little? What do you say when someone close to you suffers the unimaginable? When it's time to say goodbye to that aged parent? What do you say to a dying friend? To their relatives? To one who has just learned they have an incurable illness? To the couple who suffers a miscarriage or stillbirth? To the one whose spouse breaks their marriage vows? What can you say? How can you say anything when the very thought of what they're going through rips through your heart and your own emotions fail to cooperate?

Words escape us during these times and we feel lost, inadequate and frustrated. What can we do to help them with their immediate needs, and then later, to help them find the pieces of their puzzle? After some time has passed, should we even mention it? What if we say the wrong thing? At a time when our friends and family need us the most, words fail us. We don't know how to help and as a result, we usually don't say anything. After all, *time* is the healer, isn't it?

> **Words escape us during these times and we feel lost, inadequate and frustrated**

This study is designed to help those of us who really want to help the grieving ~ to be able to wipe their tears. Perhaps you are the one who is grieving, and these pages will enable you to let others help you. Whatever the case, I hope the pages of this book will serve you; help you to help others and in turn, strengthen us so we can honor God and give Him the glory.

Our Story

Do you remember the segment on the CBS early morning show some years ago, entitled, *Everyone has a story?* Steve Hartman would throw a dart over his shoulder and it would land at a random place on a map. He then would go to the town, open up a phone book and randomly choose a name, just to see what that person's *story* would be. Everyone has one and this is ours.

Jill Louise Jamerson

The name had a nice ring to it. We had another girl's name picked out for three babies, but they turned out to be Randy, Byron and Allen. On her date of birth, April 7, 1974, the other name didn't seem to fit, but Jill seemed just right. After an initial period of distress, due to meconium aspiration, she was a healthy little bundle of energy.

Her brothers thought she was a queen and treated her as such, often teasing her about being one. They all doted on her, adored her, and as brothers will do, pestered her. They dressed her in funny clothes, invented puppet shows, and one Christmas season wrapped her with artificial pine garlands. We had to stop them when it came time to plug her in.

She loved life and drank it all in. Each stage was a challenge and an accomplishment. Everywhere we went; people were drawn to this friendly, bubbling little ball of enthusiasm. She named Jesus as her Savior and committed her life to Him, obeying Him in baptism and influencing others with her zeal and happiness in doing right.

After the whirl of band concerts, boyfriends, and football games known as high school (oh yes, academics were in there somewhere), she was ready for college days to begin. At the hosen school with a Christian atmosphere, she delighted in being able to participate in activities with others who had also chosen to walk with God.

One enjoyable day included lunch with friends, practicing softball after classes and an impromptu volleyball game after supper. The remaining events of the day would change our lives forever.

It was September of 1993 and the details were finally all in place. My husband, Frank, was packed and ready to embark on his first teaching trip to Romania, made possible by the fall of communism. It had been a whirlwind of printing teaching materials, securing Bibles, finding a source of grape juice to be used for communion plus packing supplies and personal needs for the trip. Finally, he was off on an adventure that would last a month and would lead in many directions. What an opportunity! Our excitement was shared by the Southwest church in Lakeland, Florida where he preached and they were supporting him both materially and spiritually.

Since we had never been separated for that long, I wondered what I would do with my time for a month. We had three sons in different locations in Alabama and Jill was just beginning her second year at Florida College in Tampa. Since she lived on campus, there was no need to stay home by myself for a whole month so I was excited about my own travel plans and the opportunity to visit family. Two sons were in Dothan, the oldest was in Selma and my parents lived further north in Athens, Alabama so I intended to see them all. All the appropriate phone numbers and itinerary had been given to friends and family.

My first stop was in Dothan. Byron and Angi had moved into a new house, so I packed the sewing machine with plans to help make curtains while there. Allen and Julie were in the process of building a new house, and the foundation had just been poured. I had worked on curtains most of the day on September 16 and was ready to break the monotony by watching Byron play volleyball with his hospital league. Allen and Julie were with me, so afterward we went by their property to see what had been done that day. When I returned to Byron's house, Angi was rather upset, having received a phone call from Florida College. The information received was that Jill had collapsed after a volleyball game and had been taken to University hospital in Tampa and I was to wait there for a call from the doctor. My first thoughts were that she had become dehydrated. I had warned her many times about playing sports in the hot Florida sun, but when the doctor called, it was quite a different picture. She was unconscious due to what they thought was a cerebral hemorrhage and I should come as quickly as I could. When I questioned the doctor, his chilling comment was unsettling. *"These things don't tend to get better."* I knew then we were facing a desperate situation.

Immediately, packing began for the trip home. Leaving as soon as possible, Allen and Julie drove with me to Tampa, and upon our arrival at the hospital in the wee hours of the morning, the doctor took us into a private room to explain there was little hope for recovery. Frank had been contacted and with a few complications, was on his way home. Family arrived to join friends who were waiting with me. Early Saturday morning, September 18th, there was no more brain activity. We arranged to donate her vital organs, and that would be done after her daddy arrived, later in the day.

Four months later, the medical report revealed that she had a malignant brain tumor, a grade two astrocytoma that had hemorrhaged. We had no knowledge of this condition, and no warning. There were no previous symptoms.

Neither of us would ever speak to our daughter again and that lone phone call would forever change our lives and throw us into what is known as the grief process.

1

What is Grief, Anyway?

"Why is your face sad though you are not sick? This is nothing but sadness of heart," Nehemiah 2:2.

What would be your own personal definition of grief? In your own mind, you may have several possible definitions. The word naturally reminds us of the difficult time surrounding the loss of a loved one. It may remind us of the ravages of war and of families who have lost a leader, a son or daughter. Miscarriage or still birth brings about a unique kind of sadness that many do not understand. The loneliness of divorce, learning of life threatening illness or being a caretaker throughout illness, losing a job, dealing with disobedient children and many other situations, remind us of times of grief. We even mourn the loss of a beloved pet. Grief is the feeling of loss after an event and may be as simple as a passing moodiness or as intricate as a deep crushing agony.

The scenes of September 11, 2001 are etched in most of our minds and we remember the horrors of that day and the wrenching display of grief: disbelief, agony and deep distress. We had seen a similar display on a much lesser scale on April 19, 1995, the day that 168 people lost their lives at the hand of a madman in the Oklahoma City bombing. On the day he was executed, our local newspaper printed the photos of all those who were killed. I looked at it through tears, realizing every photo represents torn relationships and crushed dreams. Our hearts are touched with the grief of others, especially in the midst of such senseless circumstances. That page of photos is still in my files, knowing that behind each one is a special story of changed lives.

Grief is deep sorrow caused by an extreme loss. We use the words bereaved, deceased, loss, affliction, and death. We, as Christians, speak of death as a passing ~ from one life to another. Webster defines bereaved (bereft) as *to be deprived of something; left sad and lonely, as by a death.* There are many terms used synonymously for grief: sorrow, woe, tribulation sadness, trial, suffering or melancholy. The words mourn, lament, weep and moan all give us the picture of overwhelming distress. Mourning is usually the outward expression of grief and may differ according to cultural background.

Grief produces such feelings as anger, fear, regret, shame, guilt, resentment, loneliness, uselessness and a desire to die. It's extremely difficult to focus ~ on anything. Some will be so crushed they can barely function; others try to put the best face forward while in public and do their grieving privately.

Sudden death seems to complicate all of the above, making adjustment even more difficult. I would compare the grief of sudden death to being severely beaten and when your wounds need attending, those around you expect you to ignore it; to act *normal* as though nothing had happened, saying ~

Pull yourself together!

Be Happy

> *You're young ~ you can marry again or you can have other children*

> *The sooner you let go the better*

> *Take some time off*

> *Get a job*

> *Get some rest*

> *Stay busy*

Such a conflict of advice and emotions!

Upon suffering a loss, whether from long term illness or from sudden death, there will be three general stages: shock, uffering and recovery. (I've often wondered about the word recovery. It sounds as if you'll be able to return to life as it was, when in reality, you'll never be there again.) There are lots of other little stages in-between, but those are the three basic ones. For those who have been care-givers, the shock period is shorter, but it is still there. There are feelings of numbness and hopelessness. Necessary chores are accomplished only by habit. It's easy to become convinced that you are stuck in this unhappiness and will be this way forever.

Grievers vacillate between logic and emotion, and easily bounce from one to the other, depending on the circumstance. They constantly think of the lost one and cannot at first, replace those thoughts regardless of how hard they try. Most grievers will not confess all their thoughts and agonies, and silently bear much of it alone, realizing that their presence as well as their thoughts, if they reveal them, are a burden to others because most people just do not understand. Those grieving might actually try to conceal their own pain, for fear of bringing pain upon their friends, and in desperation, wonder about their own sanity. This fear leads to isolation.

> Grievers vacillate between logic and emotion, and easily bounce from one to the other, depending on the circumstance

Going about routine chores for the first time, is exactly that; the *first* time, and the first time for doing everything lasts 365 days. It is a lonely feeling. It is difficult to be in public, whether it be at church or the grocery store. Life is being lived in a cloud or a bubble, only observing and not actually participating; just going through the motions and trying to get through that day, longing for night time so hopefully sleep will come. Just when those enduring grief think they are reaching the top of the grief ladder, they fall down again and have to start over. It's a tiresome, exhausting drudgery ~ every ounce of strength seems to be gone. Eating, a normally enjoyable activity, becomes labor. Exhaustion, whether mental or physical, takes its toll on both mind and body.

C.S. Lewis said, "I never knew grief felt so much like fear." The grievers may be tempted to isolate themselves because of fear:

a) of the unknown
b) of bringing pain to their friends
c) of appearing weak or helpless
d) of losing their own sanity
e) of entering into life by themselves

There are so many variants in grief it's no wonder that many friends do not know what to do! We don't know what to say and we don't begin to know how to wipe their tears. Sometimes they're in one mood; sometimes another. Why can't they settle down? When will it ever end? Why do they talk about their loved one? Why *don't* they mention their loved one?

Remember the descriptions above and realize that grief doesn't disappear after the funeral. Daily activities are handled out of necessity and the reality of life has not yet begun. In fact, the danger period is from four to seven months following, when most friends no longer visit or send cards and expect the griever to be *over it*. The grief process does not end on a schedule. It may fade and reappear for many years in an unpredictable cycle, sometimes when it is the least expected.

It may be difficult to understand why they behave as they do. If we are patient and wait for appropriate moments, we can show our willingness to help. Quietly letting them know we are available when they want to talk is another way to bring comfort. Prepare brief questions: *Does it still make you sad to speak of _____? Whenever you are ready, I would enjoy hearing some stories of _____ (life, school, work, dreams, marriage, etc.)*

Remember, they're not only mourning the personal loss, but also the loss of relationship. It may be a spouse, son, daughter, friend, brother, sister, etc. The relationship seems to be gone. It's a rare person who doesn't love to hear stories about their loved one. Memories are made to be shared. We still enjoy seeing Jill's friends from time to time and love to hear funny *Jill* stories. She is our daughter and in our hearts, the relationship is still there. The stories are part of her. To some, the relationship is lost, unless they have sufficient memories to sustain it. She was a child, grandchild, sister, niece, cousin, friend, girlfriend, pal, acquaintance, counselor and so on. In the sweet and poignant story <u>Tuesday's with Morrie</u>,[1] one of Morrie's aphorisms is: *Death ends a life, not a relationship.* Oh, the lessons Mitch learned while caring for his old friend and mentor. It's a wonderful chronicle of caring ~ each one for the other.

Grief reactions

Shock
Numbness
Loneliness
Anger
Disoriented ~ Confused
Lack of appetite ~ Increased appetite
Hard to face friends
Want to be with people
Want to be alone
Too depressing to be with others ~ Dragging others down
Difficult to be in public
Foggy and forgetful
Emotional
Pre-occupied
Overwhelmed with legal details
Questions regarding faith
Depressed
Illness
Guilt ~ Regret
Fear

JOY
HOPE

This list, and many variations of it, appears in grief management materials and I offer my apologies for not being able to note its original source. Joy and Hope are at the bottom of the grieving list and they do qualify as grief reactions.

> ## Death ends a life, not a relationship
> ## – Morrie Schwartz

Eventually joy and hope will return, as grievers turn outward instead of inward. Progress is being made when they can reach out to help someone else, and in the process, begin to heal themselves. Laughter will eventually return and the sting of the loss will soften.

All of the above symptoms are part of the whole grieving picture, so you can see that it can be quite confusing. Men and women grieve very differently. Many women would rather discuss the situation and most men will retreat and not discuss it until they can find a solution and once again face the world. Ways to grieve and lengths of time to grieve vary according to personality, upbringing and culture. The first year was so difficult, both Frank and I silently wished we *could* hide somewhere until it had passed. In our society though, continued isolation only increases the problem. Although his book is not about grieving, John Gray points out the differences in problem solving in Men are from Mars; Women are from Venus.[2]

When a person, either male or female, just cannot talk about it, journaling may be helpful. It gets the feelings out without fear of embarrassment. (For several months, I would incessantly run details over and over in my mind, unable to control it or put them aside, until I finally wrote them all down. Was I afraid I'd forget? I don't know, but writing it all down helped solve the problem and I think I've referred to that document only once since.)

"So I said, 'Oh, that I had wings like a dove! I would fly away and be at rest. Indeed, I would wander far off, and remain in the wilderness," Psalm 55:6, 7.

Questions for study & discussion:

1. Give your own personal definition of grief.

2. Name and discuss the three general stages of grief.

3. Prepare three brief questions that would help start a conversation with a griever.

4. Can you add to the list of grief reactions?

5. Why are joy and hope at the bottom of the list of grief reactions?

6. Make a list of Bible characters who suffered the loss of family members.

THE MOST CARING CHILD

Author and lecturer Leo Buscaglia once talked about a contest he was asked to judge. The purpose of the contest was to find the most caring child. The winner was a four-year-old child whose next door neighbor was an elderly gentleman who had recently lost his wife. Upon seeing the man cry, the little boy went into the old gentleman's yard, climbed onto his lap, and just sat there. When his mother asked him what he had said to the neighbor, the little boy said, *Nothing, I just helped him cry.*[3]

2

Illness Brings Grief Too?

"How blessed is he who considers the helpless; The Lord will deliver him in a day of trouble," Psalm 41:1.

Grief comes in many forms.

I'm sorry, Mrs. Smith. You have cancer. I regret to inform you Mr. Jones, but you have heart disease; your heart is badly damaged. Many of you have either experienced those words or know someone who has. Devastating, overwhelming, disturbing words; words that make you question your security and make your future melt in front of you.

You may have heard words that are somewhat less traumatic, but still shocking and disturbing. You have chronic fatigue, fibromyalgia, lupus, a thyroid problem or some type of mental disorder. What does this involve? How am I going to deal with this? What will I do? What will my future be? Am I going to be disabled? Will people understand?

When these words are personalized, it is good to have the help of a *kindred spirit* who can educate and prepare those involved. The unknown is surely our greatest fear. We, as Christians, can teach one another just by sharing experiences and as a result, relieve some of the fear that comes with the unknown.

Thanks be to God for the sisters who have been through the breast cancer experience and have been so informative and helpful to those who have been similarly afflicted. One sister helped those around her to understand what phase of treatment she was in, why they chose that particular type treatment and some of the ups and downs that came about during that time. Mike and Cheryl Wilson permitted us to share their experience through his book, <u>Christians and Cancer</u>,[4] letting us understand not only their medical journey, but all the emotions that went long with the experience. If you want to help others, you need to read his book.

When the phone call is made to inquire about someone's ill health, make sure the call is about the person you called and not about you. It's common to share stories without thinking through to the end of the story. Did the patient in our story survive? Perhaps it would be best to share only the positive experiences ~ those who have finished treatment and have been cancer free for 5-10 years. One woman warmly told her friend who was enduring chemotherapy, that she had heard about her illness; that she knew what it was like to be worried with health issues and then proceeded to say *if you don't have your health, you have nothing.* I'm sure the patient was overjoyed to hear that! Ignorance may be bliss in some situations, but not this one. We have a duty to learn and respond in such a way that will build faith and solidify relationships.

> **Would you expect a cancer patient to cure their own cancer or a heart patient their own heart disease?**

Would you expect a cancer patient to cure their own cancer or a heart patient their own heart disease? How silly. Would you tell them to take an anti-depressant and quit stressing? Of course not. How about fatigue? Now that's another matter! Chronic fatigue is a wearisome, debilitating disease. It joins other autoimmune diseases that cannot be helped, but is hard to diagnose. Unexplained fatigue seems to bring on judgments from well meaning but thoughtless Christians as if the sufferer has to *pass the test* before he or she can receive sympathy or help. There is a lack of understanding of any illness that has no clearly visible symptoms and we're all too quick to give our opinion when we have not walked in those shoes. Chronic conditions, especially when coupled with pain, wear a person down, not only physically, but emotionally and sometimes spiritually. Pain can be brought on by stress. With more compassion, those afflicted may even recover more quickly because they know others care and they're not alone.

It's tough enough to be ill, but even more stressful to feel that no one understands or cares.

> **The paralytic in Mark had friends who went the second mile to see that he received help....**

Worry Free Living[5] by Minirth, Meier and Hawkins provides valuable insight as to how brain chemistry can be changed by stress and anxiety, with Biblical approaches to recovery.

The paralytic in Mark the second chapter, had friends who went the second mile to see that he received help, even to the point of breaking through the roof so he could see Jesus. Contrast that to the man with an infirmity in John 5, who had no friend to lower him into the pool of Bethesda. For 38 years he had this difficulty and Jesus compassionately ended his suffering. We cannot end suffering as Jesus did, but we can help to lighten the load.

May I take the kids to the playground today?
I love to iron, trim bushes, etc. May I do it for you?
What day would be best to bring your favorite casserole?

The fibromyalgia/chronic fatigue diagnosis is complicated, and once it is given, doctors tend to ignore additional symptoms saying, *you have fibromyalgia or chronic fatigue, you'll just have to live with it.* Fibromyalgia, bone pain, weakness and fatigue can be constant companions and those who deal with it daily would be certain to appreciate kind words instead of criticism. The guilt that comes about because of no longer being able to fulfill the heart's desire of visiting, hospitality or participating in teaching programs can be unbearable. Then add the pressure of not being believed or understood! Our insinuations can actually worsen the situation and bring more stress to the one who is ill. (It is not an act of selfishness to put your own needs first every now and then; in fact, quite the opposite. Time spent repairing or rebuilding health can pave the way for being even more useful in the future.)

Each of us has an inner value and we have the tools to bring out the inner value in others. We have the tools of encouragement in our hands! Will we use them?

After our son Randy's automobile accident in 1993, he was told over and over how *lucky* he was. (I really prefer *blessed*. God blessed Randy greatly that night.) After hitting a log truck at night that had no runner lights, he *did* have a narrow escape and was extremely thankful, recognizing and giving thanks for his vast array of blessings. That didn't negate the fact that he had been airlifted to a hospital in a strange city and was now in a hospital room, totally immobilized with two broken arms, a broken hip and compound fracture of the femur. He was in pain and not feeling particularly *lucky* right then! Sometimes, we just need to state the obvious. *I'm sorry you are in such pain; this is a major life change for you. Can I handle any personal details for you?* Or at least precede our remarks with *I don't mean to trivialize your pain or grief, but...you are incredibly blessed!* Gratefully, many people did attend to him, providing his every need, even spending nights with him so I could be at the hospital in the daytime while Frank took care of duties at home. Yes, he was blessed, but also grieving for his former healthy body, for his job, his home and everything else that was put on hold while he recuperated.

Stress can affect the immune system. It may be that because of the additional stress, a caretaker or one grieving the loss of a loved one may actually develop any variety of immune system disorders or become physically ill in some other way, thus complicating the recovery and increasing the need for attention. Once again, we are given the opportunity to *bear one another's burdens,* Galatians 6:2. Professionals estimate that anxiety can be cut in half just by having a good listener.

Timothy Kenny, in his book, <u>Living with Chronic Fatigue Syndrome</u> states,

> *Ignorance and fear are simply not good enough excuses for turning your back on other people when they need you most. Friends made uncomfortable by tragedy miss*

the opportunity to do good for themselves as well as for those suffering loss. We should all make the effort to step across the line of discomfort, reach out to someone who might be alone in their circumstances. It can make a world of difference for the person in need and might really make you feel good about yourself. [6]

Stressful living, whether it is from grief, caretaking or high pressure jobs, will weaken the immune system and open the pathway for autoimmune diseases. Numbers of years are often spent trying to find answers to a puzzling myriad of symptoms. My own journey took eight years and ten different doctors to eventually receive the diagnosis of Celiac disease. At that time, Celiac was one of the most under diagnosed conditions because physicians just didn't think it existed in this country. Now, it is more easily diagnosed, at least in some areas of the country. Because of muscle and bone pain, I was one of those who received the fibromyalgia diagnosis and from then on was told, *well, you're just going to ache a lot*. Unfortunately, I have both, but the celiac was being overlooked. Learning through research, I found that celiac, as well as other autoimmune conditions, can lay dormant in the genes and be triggered by trauma. Bingo!

It is extremely important to have a healthy diet plan during times of stress. A time of grieving or illness will weaken the body, so it is not a time to resort to junk food. You may be a valuable help to someone who isn't feeling up to planning and preparing meals, especially if you're knowledgeable in the area of nutrition. Anyone with food sensitivities or auto-immune conditions can receive valuable information by visiting www. livingwithout.com.

In preparing for this chapter, I asked several women who have had serious illnesses to give me their top ten memorable things that were done for them. One immediately responded, *the cards*. Every day throughout her cancer treatment, she received get well cards; some from friends and relatives and many from people she had never met. Some of the good wishes came from Christians who were participating in group meetings of their congregations. These groups meet regularly with the primary goal of encouraging and comforting.

I also asked them for the top five things they wished had never been said, and on the top of the list were comments about the loss of hair. Hair loss is such a personal thing for a woman; probably the most dreaded aspect of chemotherapy.

One rather amusing event told by a cancer patient who had hair loss because of her treatments, was when a man walked into a shopping cart because he was so busy looking at her! The same sweet sister requested that women around her tell her funny stories ~ anything to keep from being overcome with the seriousness of what was happening to her body. (Imagine sitting in the doctor's office after receiving the big C diagnosis only to be told by the doctor that *we all have to go sometime.)*

> Imagine sitting in the doctor's office after receiving the big C diagnosis only to be told by the doctor that we all have to go sometime

It does help to have a sense of humor and those who are seriously ill appreciate keeping it light! It also goes both ways. A visitor once said, *They tell me you're a little under the weather.* To which the patient replied, *You're kidding! They told me I have cancer. Do you suppose there's been a mix-up?* Fortunately, in my little survey, the negative comments were far outweighed by the positive.

In <u>The Right Way to Comfort a Friend with Cancer</u>, an article by Jennifer Allen in Good Housekeeping, April 2006, the author made this statement:

> *Think of what you're going to say. Even if we're acting plucky, we cancer patients feel fragile. It's as if we're walking around with our outer layer of skin peeled off ~ every thoughtless remark is like splashing us with lemon juice.* An appropriate comment, as a friend was telephoning was: *If you don't want to talk about it, that's*

fine ~ just tell me how you're feeling. When can I drop off the lasagna? [7]

When one dear lady lost her hair and she had to start wearing hats, many women in her congregation joined in by wearing a hat ~ even young girls.

There were foot rubs for aching bodies, bundles of bath products for soaking away aches, flowers, gift baskets, yard work, hand made blankets, clothes ironed, field trips to give small children some distraction, meals prepared and *friend sitting.* (We won't call it baby sitting.)

Who could help but be touched by the dear sister who was sick and elderly herself, but had called a friend with cancer, saying she had prayed that God would take her own life and spare hers, and she died shortly thereafter.

Another touching event was the delivery of soup ~ homemade, pre-packaged, frozen and hand delivered. The delivery involved a three hour trip one way and the two women had never met. It is a wise decision to pre-package a food delivery so that freezing is optional, in case it is not needed right away.

In another instance, women rallied around a sister who was not a patient, but was caring for her very ill husband. She stayed night and day at the hospital ~ a lonely, wearisome task. One particular time, a large basket was delivered, full of personal items, snacks, crossword puzzles, note cards, pens, stamps, body lotion, spiritual calendars and the latest issue of some magazines.

Men also enjoy this gesture, but may be harder to buy for. Many of the above suggestions, plus small personal items, handkerchiefs, fruit, home cooked goodies and inspirational reading material are suitable.

Depending on the situation, a yard work or house cleaning party may go a long way in boosting the morale of the patient or caretaker.

Completing the list, of course, were the prayers. Knowing others are praying sustains us, giving comfort and peace. Many would reveal their prayer routines and total strangers would say they were praying regularly. Never be afraid to tell someone you are praying for them. Don't just say, *I'm thinking about you.* Thinking about someone is not praying! What a comforting, strengthening thought to know that someone else has brought your name before the most powerful source of strength available.

One lady told me that as she cared for her mother, she felt lonely and isolated and wished for visitors; but when visitors came, she had things to take care of and wished they would leave. Her statement aptly described the confusing feelings of illness, caretaking and grief. Feel your way along. Even if your timing isn't perfect, the kind gesture will be long remembered.

We have the responsibility to ask how we can be of service and those who are ill have the responsibility of providing a direct answer. It's difficult to know exactly what is appropriate at any given time, but with practice we can take advantage of opportunities that we either didn't see before or felt inadequate or unprepared to help. A helpful internet resource is www.urhopeonline.com, where articles and discussion about chronic illness, death, and daily trials are found. It is edited by two Christian women who have their own afflictions and want to be of service to others.

Questions for study and discussion:

1. Remembering *a soft answer turns away wrath*, give your response to a sister who makes this comment about another sister. *Well, I'm sicker than she is, and **I** manage to come to worship services.*

2. How does helping the grieving compare to helping those who are physically sick?

3. List commonly made comments that are helpful.

4. List commonly made comments that are not helpful.

5. What helpful things would you appreciate if you became seriously ill?

3

But I Don't Know What to Say!

"Let your speech always be with grace, seasoned, as it were, with salt, so that you may know how you should respond to each person," Colossians 4:6.

The familiar passage in Ecclesiastes 3 tells us that there is a *"time to give birth and a time to die"* and later goes on to say that there also is a *"time to weep and a time to laugh; a time to mourn and a time to dance"* and also a *"time to be silent and a time to speak."* (That's the part that gives us the most difficulty ~ the knowing when to be silent and knowing when to speak).

Although Randy's automobile accident produced several broken bones, by God's grace, there were no internal injuries. After considerable time and treatment, he resumed normal activities. Now, many years later, I doubt he thinks about that accident every day, or even every week, but the scars remain. The injuries healed long ago. The redness has gone, but the scar is still there as a reminder. Grieving is the same. When dealing with a grieving person, even long after the death, we have to recognize their scars.

Some physical scars will redden with certain activity, and our grieving scars will do the same. Certain dates, certain situations, certain locations, certain music is sure to bring about a passing thought or remembrance. We should feel free to briefly mention a lost loved one to a griever. (The key word here is *briefly*). Even though it may bring tears, for most it would bring about a good feeling to know their loved one is remembered. Remember, *death ends a life, not a relationship*.

"It is better to go to a house of mourning than to go to a house of feasting, because that is the end of every man, and the living takes it to heart," Ecclesiastes 7:2.

No one is isolated from death and its effects. Scripture reminds us to *"rejoice with those who rejoice and weep with those who weep,"* Romans 12:15. Rejoicing is just more fun!

Why are we so hesitant to speak of death with a friend? It's probably because we're afraid we'll say the wrong thing and we're right! It should be a natural thing, but it is not our nature to bring up a subject that we fear might cause pain. And yet, should we let them bear that pain alone? Is not *"bear one another's burdens and so fulfill the law of Christ"* (Galatians 6:2) a good scripture? With practice, we can provide a safe place for someone who is grieving.

Perhaps we fail at comforting because we just want to give sympathy on our own terms. Do we want to say a quick word in order to do our duty and make *ourselves* feel more comfortable? A little self examination and checking of our own motives may be in order, for there are several sure ways to make them uneasy.

Ways to add to their discomfort

1. **Stay uninvolved**. Ignore the situation and do not communicate. (Most of the time we do that because we just don't know what to say.)

> Suggestion: *I want to help if you will just show me how.* Avoid *If there's anything I can do, just let me know!* Especially when grief is fresh, it is just not possible to put wants or wishes into words; to know exactly what is needed, and the strength needed to carry on with some relationships is just not there. You will have to be the aggressor in offering help or maintaining a relationship. If you're still afraid to broach the subject, the first response should be to pray ~ for the right approach, for wise words, and for the wisdom to use those words at the right time.

2. **Hover.** Sympathize and reinforce their hopelessness; use a tone of pity.

Oh, you poor thing, this is a terrible thing to happen; I don't know how you'll ever get over it. I know the same thing happened to so and so and they <u>never</u> got over it.

Suggestion: Express sympathy, but not in a way that brings attention or crowds them. Being an object of pity is not desirable. Stay light. Suggest a change of pace. *Go with me today. Can I pick you up for lunch on Thursday? Is Friday a good day to bring dinner over?* A smile, a wink, or just a hand on their arm can let them know that you are aware and willing to help.

Side story: Some time ago, we had a visitor at our Sunday morning worship; a delightfully giddy college girl, whose mannerisms reminded me of Jill. She was also the only girl in a family with three brothers. When I found that out, I asked her how she handled those three brothers, and she just laughed and immediately said, *Oh, it builds character!* I don't think she ever knew the difficulty I was having, but as we finished the conversation, the look on my face evidently told a friend who is very perceptive that something was wrong. All she said was, *You OK?* I told her I was having a Jill moment. It was a trigger reaction, and they can happen many years later. My friend was wise. Nothing more was needed at the moment. (If she had tried to sympathize and look into my eyes with sorrow, I would have just gotten worse.)

3. **Chastise them for being angry**.

Suggestion: Agree they have a right to be angry, but be a good listener and suggest directing anger properly. It's not a sin to be angry, but it's a sin to stay that way. Find a way to channel the anger; do something therapeutic. Go to the gym; find a hobby; study together what the Bible says about anger. Avoid body language that suggests disapproval; having a friend who won't get all out of joint if you express anger is a valuable friend, indeed. A friend with whom you can discuss the very pits of life without being criticized is a rare treasure. Do we need to work on being that type of friend? If anger *is* expressed, let your friend get it out of his or her system. Ask if there's anything else that needs to be said, and if not, express that you understand. *Fine then, now that you've gotten that out of your system, let's go walking.* Or whatever activity you think may be appropriate. No chastisement or condemnation is needed. Choose a distracting activity, but realize that the griever may not be ready to visit the sick or a patient in the hospital. While waiting with a friend whose father was having surgery, I realized I did not need to be there. It was agony. The hospital experience was just too fresh.

4. **Assure them that Christians have no right to be depressed.**

Really? Have you studied Moses, Elijah or Job lately? Good people do experience depression! In Numbers 11, read the (paraphrased) words of Moses, speaking to God. *"Why are you treating me like this? I am so troubled! Have I failed you so badly that you 'dump on me' with all these people? I'm not their parent! I didn't conceive them. So why do I have to take care of them? I just don't get it! Where will we find food? They're driving me absolutely nuts with their complaining! This is too much. Why don't you just kill me and get it over with!"* Moses was *coming apart at the seams* because he was so overburdened and God, through Jethro, found a way to lessen that burden. Through you, your friend's burden can also be lessened. First, give it time and if it continues, find the source of the depression. Depression can be from sin, chemical imbalances, or it can be just temporary.

5. **Show your impatience.** Tell them they need to get over it.

Suggestion: Remind them with compassion that grieving takes a while. After the sudden death of my sister-in-law, my brother's doctor told him, *You're going to go through* *a lot of <u>stuff</u> I can't help you with, but if you start feeling hopeless about it all, or unable to sleep, I <u>can</u> help you. Point out that waiting is an art.* When David was chosen by God to be the next king and anointed in 1 Samuel 16, he went right into office ~ right? Wrong. He had a giant to attend to as well as a very cranky King Saul. Saul was permitted to chase David around for 14 years! Doesn't that seem like a waste? Surely, God could have used David in better service. Waiting, and doing the right thing while doing so is not easy and David had to wonder about God's plan for him. But without this experience, would we have seen David's beautiful feelings captured in the Psalms? Would we have seen his agony? Or his wonderful words of praise?

Remind them of their blessings.

It really is no comfort to be told how blessed you are because many other people have suffered greater things. Right at this moment, the pain is intense! Counting blessings will come later. Instead, ask *what was your happiest time together? What is your favorite memory? You took such good care of and did everything possible for* _____. Be positive in asking leading questions and let them talk. Don't try to *fix* it. Be prepared to <u>listen</u>, comfort and wipe a few tears.

> Be prepared to listen, comfort and wipe a few tears

The first duty of love is to listen ~ Paul Tillich

Get lots of rest ~ Stay busy.

Well, isn't that a paradox! But look what God did for Elijah. After the contest with Baal and the threat on his life by Jezebel, Elijah was worn out. God provided rest and food. He was first fed by a widow (1 Kings 17:13-

16) and then by an angel (1 Kings 19:5-8) and then he got busy (More on that later). Scripture teaches us to wait, to rest, and to receive proper nourishment before moving on.

8. Change the subject.

Grievers can be puzzled by the reaction of others. Some seem to be sympathetic and others just want to change the subject. Expressing sorrow seems to be taboo among many Christians. Instead of *I'm sorry to hear that* and then changing the subject, try *I'm sorry to hear that. This must be so painful. What can I do? May I help you with...?* It's perfectly all right to ask them if this is a good time to talk about it, providing the occasion and surroundings are right. Timing is important, as is privacy.

If we really want to help, we simply must learn to speak about death. Because it's difficult to talk to a dying person, we tend to avoid the subject and just ask others how he or she is doing. Going the distance and being a true friend is time consuming! Helping a friend who is facing a serious illness is tricky. On Death and Dying[8] is a very informative book by Elizabeth Kubler Ross and a must read for anyone who is dealing with those who are terminally ill. When we lived in Florida, the mother of a Christian there was dying. It was a very difficult situation, in that she had suffered a series of medical complications that compounded rather than alleviated problems. We knew, and she knew, that she was going to die. This wonderful woman made it easy for those around her to comfort her. One young Christian worked at the hospital and had many opportunities to visit and pray with her. The knowledge and comfort gained from this experience was invaluable to both parties, but never would have taken place without the courage of the young Christian.

Another friend at church developed a difficult form of cancer. Instead of withdrawing and feeling sorry for herself, he kept us all informed of her progress, explaining, sometimes in detail, the medical procedures that were being used and the hope for recovery. Her expression *either way, it's going to be fine* was an uplifting light to many of us. Hope was abundant, joy for us and a wonderful aid to a speedy recovery.

Clipped from a <u>Dear Abby</u> column was this story. As a daughter cared for her mother, the mother asked, *am I dying? Her wise and caring answer ~ I don't know. But let's do whatever we need to do as if you were. Let's talk and share; then if you don't die, we'll be all the richer.* Her mother died two years later. I cannot help but wonder how much those healing words had to do with her lifespan.

Some are just ill equipped to speak of anything painful, and try to avoid the subject. We need practice in dealing with this situation so comfort can be offered to that struggling person sitting a few pews away. It does get easier! Others are afraid if they sympathize, it will encourage the griever to stay in that place of grief just to get attention. Only in rare cases would that be true. Grievers do come to the realization that the choice to live again is also to risk more pain, but grief is not a good place to be, and most would love to have distraction from it, realizing the need to be a working part of society.

> **Some are just ill equipped to speak of anything painful, and try to avoid the subject**

Our words can be destructive or they can be healing. One man told my husband that he knew what it was like to lose a child, for he had read about David in the Bible. We had read of David too, but that certainly didn't prepare us for losing a child.

"A person's words can be life giving water, words of true wisdom are as refreshing as a bubbling brook," Proverbs 18:4.

"A truly wise person uses few words…," Proverbs 17:27.

In order to say encouraging words, we need a little insight and understanding for each situation. Our friend, Roger, wrote down some of his feelings after his wife died, specifically so he could help his friends understand what he was going through. Some grief support groups use similar material. Leaving out personal references, here are his thoughts.

Things I wish I could tell people about my grief

1. I wish you would not be afraid to speak her name. She lived, and was important to me. I need to hear her name.
2. If I cry or become emotional when we talk about her, I want you to know that it isn't because you have hurt me. The fact that she died has caused my tears. You have allowed me to cry and I thank you. Crying and emotional outbursts are healing.
3. I will have emotional highs and lows, ups and downs. I wish you wouldn't think that if I have a good day, my grief is all over, or that if I have a bad day, I need psychiatric counseling.
4. I wish you knew that all of the *crazy* grief reactions I am having are in fact very normal. Depression, anger, frustration, and hopelessness are to be expected following the death of a loved one.
5. I wish you wouldn't expect my grief to be over in six months. The first few years are going to be exceedingly traumatic for me. As with an alcoholic, I will never be *cured* or a *former bereaved person*, but will forevermore be a *recovering bereaved person*.
6. I wish you understood the physical reactions to grief. I may gain weight or lose weight ~ sleep all the time or not at all ~ develop a host of illnesses and be accident prone, all of which may be related to my grief.
7. Her birthday, the anniversary of her death, and holidays are terrible times for me. I wish you could tell me that you are thinking about her on those days, and if I get quiet and withdrawn, just know I am thinking about her too and don't try to coerce me into being cheerful.

8. I wish you would not offer me drugs to ease my pain. These are just temporary crutches and the only way I can get through this grief is to experience it. I have to hurt before I can heal.

9. I wish you understood that grief changes people. I am not the same person I was the moment before she died and I never will be that person again. If you keep waiting for me to get back to my old self, you will be frustrated. I am a new creature with new thoughts, dreams, aspirations, values and beliefs. Please try to get to know the new me ~ maybe you will still like me. [9]

> **I wish you understood that grief changes people**

As in any area of life, if you don't know what to say, it's better to just say nothing. Friendship can still be offered by just being there. Do you remember what Solomon asked for after becoming King of Israel? God appeared to him in a dream and told him to ask for anything he wanted. He asked for a listening heart; a hearing or understanding heart, 1 Kings 3:9. Many grievers are not asking for solutions, they would just like to be heard; just needing someone to listen.

Let's call that quality listening. It reminds me of the story about a little girl who was afraid of the dark. Her mother gently told her that she wasn't alone; Jesus was with her and would help her. Her answer? *I know, Mommy, but right now I need someone with skin.*

If a negative thought arises, try to reserve judgment and consider the response, *Can you put into words why you feel that way?* Be a good listener. Anger, frustration, and hopelessness may be expressed but remember, you can thank them for being open and sharing their thoughts. Sharing is learning. Then you can enjoy being together while you work on a project, go to the store, or go to visit friends.

"He who guards his mouth and his tongue, guards his soul from troubles," Proverbs 21:23.

Questions for study and discussion:

1. Role play some destructive words and some healing words. Decide which ones you'd rather hear.

2. Just a few months after losing her son in a tragic auto accident, as women are visiting together after a worship service, a friend gets teary. Someone says, *I thought you'd be over that by now.* Give your response.

3. Briefly discuss the depression of Moses, Job and Elijah.

4. What things could be included when visiting those in affliction? James 1:27.

5. Discuss the importance of listening.

To One in Sorrow

Let me come in where you are weeping, friend,
And let me take your hand.
I, who have known a sorrow such as yours,
Can understand.
Let me come in ~ I would be very still
Beside you in your grief;
I would not bid you cease your weeping, friend,
Tears bring relief.
Let me come in ~ I would only breathe a prayer,
And hold your hand,
For I have known a sorrow such as yours,
And understand.

From *Songs of Hope* by Grace Noll Crowell [10]

4

P.J.'s, Chocolate and Mac & Cheese

"This is my comfort in my affliction, that Thy word ha
revived me," Psalm 119:50.

What does comfort mean to you? Is it visions of
fireplace, a good book and a cup of hot chocolate? How abou
cozy pajamas and an old movie? To some, snuggling up o
the couch with a purring kitten would be soothing; to other
(such as my husband), it would be an irritation. Comfort is ver
closely related to contentment. In this context, being comforte
is usually external; something that happens to you or for yo
by someone else while contentment comes from within.

Any parent can understand the power of comfort
Memories of being comforted (or not being comforted) as
child help to form our own ability to comfort others. If w
received it ourselves, it's easier to give to those around us
The ultimate comfort is found in Scripture, in 2 Corinthians 1
the well known comfort passage.

" Blessed be the God and Father of our Lord Jesus
Christ, the Father of mercies and God of all comfort, who
comforts us in all our affliction so that we may be able to
comfort those who are in any affliction, with the comfort
with which we ourselves are comforted by God. For just
as the sufferings of Christ are ours in abundance, so also
our comfort is abundant through Christ. But if we are
afflicted, it is for your comfort and salvation, or if we are
comforted, it is for your comfort, which is effective in the
patient enduring of the same sufferings which we also
suffer, and our hope for you is firmly grounded, knowing
that as you are sharers of our sufferings; so also you are
sharers of our comfort," 2 Corinthians 1:3-7.

God comforts us so we can comfort others. That's th
cycle. When our son Allen, his wife Julie and I arrived at Universit

hospital in Tampa, after driving all night from Dothan, we were actually shocked to see so many friends waiting there. They had been there most of the night, and as the day continued, more friends came to wait with me, not only for news of Jill's condition, but for my husband to return from overseas. There was a blur of phone calls, arrangements and details that made the hours pass. Forever in my memory, are those who were so attentive and compassionate. (I'm sure they all had something else to do that day). I remember thinking this is the Lord's church in action; praying, giving, sharing, doing whatever needed to be done. Prayers were offered, food appeared, drinks were brought in; items forgotten in the rush of packing were purchased.

> I remember thinking this is the Lord's church in action; praying, giving, sharing, doing whatever needed to be done

Job called his friends miserable (or sorry) comforters in Job 16:2. They just didn't understand what Job needed at the time and were not able to ease his pain. It's easy to think we know what another person needs when we've never been there. Job even said, "*Is there no limit to windy words? I too, could speak like you, if I were in your place," verse 4.* Clearly, his pain continued and the subjects that his friends addressed did not relieve his anxieties. He was not eased by their words.

Some of our comments to the grieving may be an effort to get them to put it all behind so that *we* can be more comfortable. Some time ago, a friend where we worshipped nursed his wife through a difficult illness and they lost the battle. She had been a steady ray of light to those around her, not only in her manner of life, but in the way she handled this life threatening illness. With heavy medication, she was able to continue to worship with her church family. Our friend had been under untold stress during this experience and often, as he made announcements or served in a public way during services, he would mention her sacrificial spirit and how we all needed to develop this. As it had been more than two years since her death, I didn't really understand why he continued to do this and one day, mentioned to him that I thought somewhere there must be a time of closure. He stopped doing it. I came to realize much later that I had robbed him of a very important part of his healing process. Our comments can reveal our own insecurities. Sadly, my motive was not one of helping. Being ignorant about grief, my motive was born from my own insecurity, because his comments made me uncomfortable. We are not to remove comfort ~ we are to give it!

> Years ago, problems were shared around a quilting frame or at a canning party....

We have been programmed to think in certain terms about grief. Having the right attitude and finding the right words will take practice and we will make mistakes along the way.

Authors John James and Frank Cherry point out in The Grief Recovery Handbook,[1] that our childhood can shape our feelings about grief. If you lost an item, what was a likely response? *Don't worry, honey, it can be replaced.* If the family pet died, what was the solution? *Don't worry, we'll find another one.* If your boyfriend broke up with you, what was one of mom's favorite expressions? *Don't worry, honey, there's plenty of other fish in the sea.* All these responses teach us to hide our feelings and bury our grief. This can set a pattern for the way we grieve and for our ability to help *"bear one another's burdens,"* Galatians 6:2.

Years ago, problems were shared around a quilting frame or at a canning party but we've lost the group support that automatically comes with that type society. We may be in the information age, but we don't have that intimate communication now. Cell phones indicate a kind of *hurry up* existence. We want to help, just so it is within a certain time frame. Helping a grieving friend takes time and commitment. As one gentleman helped a friend with a bipolar disorder, he said it took a year out of his life but the results were well worth it. That was dedication!

We don't want to be sorry comforters, as were Job's friends. Some of our expressions can be anything but comforting, or even worse, contrary to Scripture. Consider the following statements:

God just needed another angel to help Him.

Did He really? God doesn't need another angel. He has a heaven full of them and can call on them for assistance. There is no Biblical evidence that a deceased person becomes an angel. Lazarus, in Luke 16, was not an angel, but he was carried to heaven by angels. Psalm 148 tells us that angels were created and established for ever and ever.

This is God's will.

Why was it God's will? Why would it be God's will that my child die? Or your child? Or your loved one? Before we make God the villain we need to give credit where it is due and apply it to Satan. He's the one responsible for death and suffering. Please think before placing blame on God. Imagine the negative impact, especially on children.

God wanted your loved one more than you did.

Another assault against God! Due to complications at birth, Jill spent 10 days in the high risk nursery and a doctor actually said to us, *God may want this baby more than you do.* I know he was trying, in his own way, to warn us of the possibility of death, but had we not been Christians, that comment would hardly make us feel warm and fuzzy toward God! It would be easier to hear *they may go to be with God* or *they're with God now* ~ a true statement without blaming God.

I know just how you feel.

Please, don't ever say that. Even if you have lost a child, the situation would not be the same; no two losses are the same. Consider developing the habit of saying *I've been in a somewhat similar situation and these are the things that helped me.*

Let go ~ Move on ~ Put it behind you.

These statements are intended to be constructive, and they can be if properly timed, but it's totally contrary to what is felt in the first few months. However rational or irrational, the fear of forgetting important details is very pronounced. A griever does not *want* to forget and tries to hold on to every detail.

How are we to let go? We are to let go in the sense that we can put this tragedy into its proper place in life and continue living. Because we live and enjoy living does not mean we have no care for the deceased. Are we to let go of our loved one's memory? That's impossible. The part of our loved one that lives in our hearts will stay. Forever. We have three wonderful, compassionate and caring sons, but don't expect me to say I have three children, because I have four. Even if she has already passed on, she is still cherished and remembered.

You know ____ would not want you to act like you are acting.
A caring friend made this comment, but I had no concept of how I was acting! Never have I known such overwhelming sadness. My sense of humor was gone; nothing was funny. I only pretended to laugh at someone's jokes. Living in a cloud is depressing and certainly not desirable but I couldn't get rid of the cloud. Medication only worsened the situation, not to mention the physical and mental stress of just trying to stay balanced.

Some are anxious to say *life goes on ~ put it behind you and move on,* hoping the griever will be influenced to return to a normal life. If a griever continues to struggle, it may help to assure them that putting the past behind does not mean forgetting. It means getting to a place where memories are happy. The comment, *while you're going on with your duties in life, I know ____ still holds a special place in your heart,* not only sympathizes but places emphasis on returning to daily life.

Now that you have another child/grandchild, it makes up for losing your child.
Often we fail to understand the grief of those around us. Another child may provide excitement, love and joy that had once been lost, but it does not make up for a previous loss nor

oes it help them to deal with their true feelings. Children can, in some situations, be reminders of what is lost but time will soften that feeling and life once again becomes enjoyable.

You're young, you can have other children.

Can you imagine this being a comfort to someone who is still grieving over a miscarriage or a stillbirth? *I don't want another baby; I wanted THIS baby!* All hopes and dreams for this precious child have been crushed and the parents ~ both parents ~ have been left to deal with something over which they had no control. Don't neglect siblings and don't neglect the dad; dads are grieving, too.

> I'm sure God will do the very best thing

Are you going to have other children?

That's a very personal question. It doesn't matter how many additional children a family might have. Added children will bring joy, for sure, but the lost child will never be replaced.

Isn't it a shame that your loved one never became a Christian.

A family who has reason to question their loved one's salvation has enough to deal with, without this observation. Thankfully, the responsibility of consigning anyone to their eternal destiny belongs only to God. While in this situation many years ago, my dad made a comment that I'll always remember. *I'm sure God will do the very best thing.* And He will. Regardless of the circumstances of the death, God *will* do the very best thing. He knows the angst of a teenage mind; He knows the trouble of a suicidal mind; He knows the distorted thinking of an aging mind. He knows. Whatever the situation may be; He knows and will do what is just.

"God knows our frame...," Psalm 103:14.

And then, there's the silence.

After a couple of weeks away, when Frank and I returned home, we were greeted and welcomed home by caring friends who would have done anything possible to help us. Strangely, we could feel the tension in the atmosphere. The subject of Jill's death was certainly off limits. Some did not want to mention her for fear of our reaction. Without making a conscious decision, both of us would mention Jill in conversation just to let them know we weren't going to crumble if her name was mentioned and it gradually became easier. Even now, Jill is still a part of our conversations. Mentioning her is as natural as mentioning any of our sons. Even new friends will eventually know a little about Jill.

Words can be as a salve to a wound, or they can open that wound even more and make it more difficult to heal. We want to say the *right* thing; to have our words be an encouragement and strength. We want to *give* the comfort that is expressed in Second Corinthians 1:4, "*to comfort those who are in any trouble, with the comfort with which we ourselves are comforted by God,*" NIV. The ultimate comfort comes from God. Scripture is filled with God's comfort of His people. Even when our words fail, we can go to His Word at any time for solace.

Some time ago, at a friend's house, I found a lovely little book entitled, Silver Boxes[12] by Florence Littauer. It's based on Ephesians 4:29 which states, "*Let no unwholesome word proceed from your mouth, but only such a word as is good for edification according to the need of the moment, that it may give grace to those who hear.*"

The author wrote the book after being asked to teach a children's Bible class on the spur of the moment. She was telling the children about the verse, describing to them the importance of good words ~ words that can uplift others; words that are a blessing and not a discouragement or a curse. The children chimed in with their descriptions of what special words should be, and together they decided that our words should be as a gift to one another. One small child jumped up and said, *I know! Words should be like a present! Like silver boxes with a bow on top!*

This friend has beautifully wrapped silver boxes strategically placed in her home, just to remind her that her words are important. I like that. It's a visual lesson that sticks.

Many years ago, a dear friend died as the result of injuries suffered in an automobile accident. Opal was an older woman, without children, who had been a steady light for me as a young preacher's wife. Her life had been rather sad by most standards, losing her only child at birth; divorcing a husband who wouldn't permit her to live as a Christian. Her job and caring for her mother filled her time, as well as helping those around her after her mother died. Some evenings she would call when my husband would be out of town and ask if she could come over and visit. I was always happy to have her company, and she understood that I would be interrupted with baths, homework and questions from our four young children. She would bring her needlework and we would fit conversation into any spare moments. Even though we lived in a different city when I heard of her death, I felt such sadness, not only because of the suddenness of it, but because I remembered good times in her company and silently grieved the loss of those times. Someone commented to me in passing how merciful God was to this woman, as she was growing old, and had no family to care for her.

That comment was a silver box ~ exactly what I needed. It put me in the proper frame of mind, thanking God for her life and influence. By God's grace, she would be happier and at peace.

"Like apples of gold in settings of silver is a word spoken in right circumstances," Proverbs 25:11.

Having been the recipient of so many valuable words ~ words that stayed in our hearts to comfort and encourage us as we faced our loneliness and sadness, we are now even more aware of the importance of our words. Some were spoken, some were written but I still struggle for that word that *gives grace to the hearer*. Sometimes we grasp for words, not realizing the power of just being quietly there and as a result, we say things that do not give grace. One fear in trying to write this book is that some will think we always say or do

the right thing. Believe me, Frank and I still struggle with that.
Every grief situation is different.

Through the pages of this book, I so hope you will find
some words that will be *good for edification according to the
need of the moment* and that through our study together we
can happily speak of those who have departed and lose our
fear of helping those who are grieving, realizing that only in
heaven will all of our questions finally be answered.

Please Dear Friend

Please, Dear Friend,
Don't say to me the old clichés,
Time heals all wounds,
God only gives you as much as you can bear,
Life is for the living...
Just say the thoughts of your heart.
I'm sorry, I love you, I'm here, I care.

Hug me and squeeze my hand.
I need your warmth and strength.
Please don't drop your eyes when I am near.
I feel so rejected now by God and man.
Just look in my eyes, and let me know that you are with me.
Don't think you must always be strong for me.

It's OK to cry.
It tells me how much you care.
Let me cry, too.
It's so lonely to always cry alone.
Please keep coming by even after many weeks have passed.
When the numbness wears off,
The pain of grief is unbearable.
Don't ever expect me to be quite the same.
How can I be when part of my being is here no more?
But please know, dear friend,
With your love, support and understanding,
I will live and love again and be grateful every day that I have
you. [13]

Mary Bailey

Questions for study and discussion:

1. When were Job's friends not comforting and what should we learn from that?

2. When we think we cannot manage, consider Paul's comment in Philippians 4:19: *"And my God shall supply all your need according to His riches in glory by Christ Jesus"*. Does this apply to the one who is comforting, the griever or both?

3. Discuss the dangers of ascribing tragedies to God.

4. David truly understood his source of comfort. Read Psalm 145:17, 18 and find other comforting passages in the book of Psalms.

5. Apply Joshua 1:9 to any current situation that is stressful.

6. Brainstorm together and try an experiment. When the deceased is mentioned, what happens? Do you freeze up? What reaction do you expect? Does the comment reflect joy or sadness? How do you react? Should you ignore it or should you sympathize? If you ignore it, what reaction would that have for the griever? What reaction would sympathy have? Which is better?

Encourage Me, Please

"Like apples of gold in settings of silver is a word spoken in right circumstances," Proverbs 25:11.

Some people just seem to have the right words at the right moment, and then there are those of us who really have to work at it!

A word, a note, a prayer straight from the heart, can carry us through a time of sorrow. Think of all the beautiful poetry that has been written during times of sorrow. Somewhere in this chapter, I hope there is a *just what you need* comment or an idea that will help you connect with a grieving friend; ideas that will help you wipe the tears of others in the grieving process. We were away from home for almost two weeks after Jill's burial, and when we picked up the mail there were almost two large postal trays of mail waiting. It took us about seven hours to open all that mail and for the next six weeks, we received mail every day.

There are many ways to connect with grieving friends. Friends, relatives and many others who were touched by the suddenness of her death were sharing in our sorrow. There are numbers of churches that have group meetings designed to encourage others and if there's any doubt as to the influence of those groups, just read on. Just the thought of that many people remembering us and mentioning our names in prayer was unforgettable. Some individuals sent poems. Some sent tapes; others sent daily message calendars and later, one friend sent a copy of *Chicken Soup for the Grieving Soul*.[14] Pages of stamps fell out of some cards and a few even included a check to help defray extra expenses. Jill and I shared a birthday and every year for three or four years, one of her high school friends sent me flowers ~ one of the most touching gestures I've ever experienced.

Every card was important and appreciated. Some notes were written on business letterheads or legal pads; even scrap paper. We treasured every word as friends poured out their hearts. I couldn't bear to part with some of those cards, especially the ones that contained personal and special thoughts. The cards have been kept in two large notebooks and on a few dark days, I've reread those encouraging words. Many of the following comments were taken from these cards. It could be that you have helped to write this chapter and the sharing of these words will bring comfort and solace to unknown faces.

> Some notes were written on business letterheads or legal pads; even scrap paper

At times, we just do not know what to say or how to say it and are unsure if we should say anything at all. The writer of Proverbs painted such a beautiful picture when he described *apples of gold in settings of silver*. Good words spoken at the right moment can comfort and influence us. Leaving out personal references, it is my prayer that sharing these words will help you give comfort to someone close to you when they are going through a difficult time. Giving comfort has to be practiced. It's the same as any other skill in our daily walk. We need practice.

> Good words spoken at the right moment can comfort and influence us

Because Jill had named Jesus as her Savior, many of these messages were written with the hope of salvation. But how do we comfort those who seem to be without hope? Some of these same messages can be used, focusing on good things in the life of the deceased and the adjustment of those left behind, leaving judgment to the righteous Judge for all time.

"Let no unwholesome word proceed from your mouth, but only such a word as is good for edification according to the need of the moment, that it may give grace to those who hear," Ephesians 4:29.

To any grieving person

I understand no one else can feel the depth of your loss. I pray for you daily. _____ means a lot to a lot of people. I'm sure everyone has their own special memories. Mine is:_____.

Please remember how much we care. We will continue to pray for all of you. I wish I could somehow wave a magic wand and fill the gap that has been left in your life.

We weep with you and *remember you without ceasing* both in our public and private prayers.

I searched and searched for the right card and then delayed writing it because I didn't know what to say. _____ was such a special person and will be missed by so many. I just want you to know I share in your sorrow.

Words cannot express the sorrow I feel at the tragic loss of _____. May the Lord bless you and comfort you and may you be sustained by your faith. May God's merciful love, caring friends, and time diminish your sorrow and make room for joyous memories.

The greatest consolation I had when dealing with the loss of my mother was that just because she had died, I didn't have to stop loving her. Once I gave myself permission to continue loving her, my pain eased.

If you can find any comfort in the words of condolence that come from the people who truly love you and the work that you have done and continue to do, then please find comfort in the knowledge that you are continually in my prayers and thoughts.

We have felt many tragedies in our work for the Lord, but few have compared to the keen sense of loss that we now feel and because of this, we send our deepest sympathy. As body and mind grow stronger, you can now be in a position of being a blessing to others in a greater measure than ever.

I am confident that the Lord in His mercy is helping significantly to bear your burden. Many faithful are going to the Lord for you.

Not a day has passed since _____'s leaving us that you are not in my thoughts and I wish so much there was something I could say to help ease your pain and loss. It pains me to think of your sadness and I can't even imagine your grief.

Sweet thoughts from young people

I might be too young to help but if you just need to talk to someone just call me, I will listen.

I'm sure the angels are having a blast with _____ around! We're praying for you and if you ever need someone to listen, I'll be there.

I often think of _____. Her memory is a great encouragement. I am very thankful I was blessed with the limited time we had. I am also thankful I can share with you these feelings. May the Lord comfort you all and strengthen you.

It's so hard to accept the fact that she is gone. My heart feels very sad and it is a funny feeling.

_____ will always be a special person to me! She blessed my life with so many of her wonderful qualities. She taught me that even when problems arise, just smile and keep on laughing and no one will know the difference. I am happy for her because she is in a better place, but I grieve with all of you. You are in my prayers.

When you can't be there

This news has broken our hearts. Our prayers are with all of you. Wish we could come and hug you all and tell you face to face how much we care.

No doubt the multitude of friends whom you have seen and heard from in the days since _____'s death have said all there is to say and all have wished for words which would not come. But we want to add our assurance of love, sympathy, and most of all prayers. Every day since the news came, your names have been mentioned above all when I prayed. We are so very sorry for your loss.

After hearing about _____ I wanted so badly to come to be with you. I attempted to write on several occasions but could not put into words the feelings in my heart. I decided to write this note, knowing our friendship could cover my inadequacy in written language.

To grieving parents

Thank you for bringing _____ up the way God wanted children raised.

_____ was a good example to me. She knew right from wrong and did an excellent job of choosing the proper path to take.

_____ was an honor to both of you. She was a joy to everyone who knew her. Her years were few but the memories will never pass.

When _____ spoke of you both, she always seemed to be talking of her best friends. I really admire that.

.....I guess what I'm trying to say is, I love you enough to want you to know that I care and want to spew out enough words that in them all a little comfort may come for you.

I could tell _____ was full of joy and life. All children have their joy but some come with that special something that lights up your life. If there is any comfort, try to remember the joy _____ gave you. _____ was a very special person who touched a lot of people's lives.

Our prayers, thoughts and tears have flowed in your behalf.

Words are not enough, nothing is; only our faith can sustain you in this time of both sadness and victory. We have all been made mindful of the brevity of life.

For those with the hope of salvation

It is difficult to think of _____'s premature departure from us without considering Enoch. Both pleased God, left the world before a normal life span and both will long be remembered with loving thoughts. For all of us, the blessed assurance that _____ will spend eternity with God is comforting.

_____'s last day wasn't her last. It was her first in the presence of her God. How great is our God! How blessed you are to know _____ is in the presence of the Almighty.

Because _____ lived and because _____ died at this time, a legacy was left for others ~ to focus their eyes more closely on our Lord.

What can we say to comfort you? If we were only there to give you hugs and shed some tears with you. If anyone is prepared for such sudden loss, we as Christians are. We have our faith and hope in God's promises, without which our hearts would break.

I'm sure we will all miss _____ but at least we have the *hope for the evidence of things not seen.* We will put our trust in the Lord Almighty to take care of _____ according to His will.

We cannot begin to imagine how you must feel at this time. Your entire family has been constantly in our prayers. We know how much we loved _____ and how much she touched our lives ~ not just because she was a joy to be around but also for the stand she took on this earth as a Christian. Not only did she not hide her light, she was a beacon showing people the way to salvation.

Now is the time to let those you have helped in the Lord return that love to you at this testing of faith. The Lord Jesus Christ will not desert you at this time. Hold fast to the confession of your hope without wavering, and you will be comforted in Him and in His Word.

We pray that the love of so many and the precious hope we have in Jesus Christ can fill a small part of the emptiness you feel right now. May the God of peace and comfort guard your hearts.

Precious friends ~ We have just heard of your loss. You are in our thoughts and prayers. We know that Heaven is a much brighter, happier place now and we, with you, have one more reason to look forward to going there.

Know that at this moment our God is looking down upon you in all His tender mercy and extending His unlimited love and compassion and mercy and care and comfort and strength and encouragement ~ to sustain you during this most difficult time in your life. He knows when His children are hurt and all caring expressions of His love are to be used in our healing process.

Special words to the deceased:

A couple of letters were written as though they were writing to Jill. One is a particular treasure. What a novel way of remembering special times and saying what you had always wanted to say.

I write this letter to your memory ~ of all the wonderful times we shared. I never really got to tell you how much I admire you. You always encouraged me to reach for my potential and the beautiful parts of life. You were always such an example of delight in life: talent, strength, humility and confidence. You could reach out and light up someone's day with a sincere compliment.

Even though you can no longer hear the songs of birds and see the beauty of each sunrise ~ I know you can hear the chorus of angels and see the glory of our Heavenly Father. I feel blessed to have known you. It is my prayer that I am remembered as you are.

On an anniversary

We just wanted to let you know that we were thinking of you on the one year anniversary of _____'s death. You're in our prayers. We miss her!

On this day of remembering, I hope it can help a little to know that others are remembering too. Our thoughts and prayers continue to be with you. For even with the passing of time the reality of the pain and void you feel as a result of _____'s death is I'm sure an ever present reminder. We can't begin to know the depth of grief involved in losing one so precious, our child. We can however continue to remember you to the One who understands all things. We pray that our Father of compassion will continue to mend your broken hearts and grant you courage and peace. May we all be encouraged to press on to higher ground as we wait for that sweetest of all reunions when we are all *safely home*.

I had seen this card and it made me think of _____. I'm sure her death is something that even now is still most difficult for you to deal with. Without a hope like ours in Christ, how <u>do</u> people get through it?

These words have meant more than I can ever say.

Writing a letter to the griever may be a good solution in these situations:

a) If there are things you want to say but cannot trust your own emotions while saying them.
b) You can say what's in your heart without causing a meltdown in a public place. It gives the griever privacy.
c) The letter can be read and re-read as needed to gain hope and strength.

Practice. There are several good books that deal with letter writing for all occasions. Check your local library or book store, or search Amazon books with key words *letter writing*.

Several good choices will appear. Some, after reading letter writing suggestions, just become intimidated and feel their words aren't *pretty* enough. Any words of compassion and hope are valuable. Don't put off sending a condolence because you don't have a pretty card. Say what is in your heart and it will be appreciated regardless of proper form. Believe me; out of the hundreds of cards we received, we were not inspecting them for grammar and form! Those words were so precious and each expression of sympathy gave comfort.

Giving comfort has to be practiced

Although it wasn't written at this particular time of grief, I'd like to share one other expression of sympathy. My dad died on December 28, 2000. We were visiting my parents and our son who had moved nearby, for the holidays. We never dreamed our trip would include funeral plans, but when we arrived, it was obvious that daddy wasn't well and had to be hospitalized. He died four days later. Frank had to return home, but I stayed to be with my mom for a couple of weeks. While there, a dear friend sent me this note:

From all you have ever spoken of your father, it is plain to see he was greatly respected and I am certain you were so special to him! I am so grateful for the man of great character your father must have been for he gave those great qualities to one of the most wonderful friends I've ever known.

I was deeply touched, not only because I valued her opinion of me, but because she recognized a special trait in my dad. Obviously, her *silver box* meant a great deal to me, or I wouldn't have kept it for so long.

"Pleasant words are a honeycomb, sweet to the soul and healing to the bones," Proverbs 16:24.

My effort to comfort a friend, newly widowed in early 1994.

Dear _____,

My thoughts come to you often. Grief comes in so many stages and it's difficult to predict just how each stage will arrive. Many times I've looked back, with thankfulness, to the protection that comes from God when we cannot handle the full force of what is happening. The shock doesn't allow us to face it all at once.

You, as we, are probably daily still adjusting. I thought that some family difficulties some years ago were my largest hurdle. I was wrong. I've never had anything shake me more severely than Jill's death. For the last couple of months, I've been better, but just yesterday I went into the drugstore, saw one of Jill's high school classmates and talked with her briefly. She was so pretty and it struck me so forcefully. I suddenly wondered what Jill would look like now and left the store in tears.

I've spent many days just trying to pass time, hoping that when night came; I could sleep and at least say one more day had passed. A good bit of time has been spent reading things connected to grief and the grief response. Aside from aged grandparents, I've never lost anyone close to me. Randy gave me a book for Christmas entitled, When God doesn't make sense[15] by James Dobson. It's good and is written from a spiritual viewpoint. I am currently reading Homer Hailey's book on Prayer and Providence.[16] Many scriptures are helpful, especially 2 Corinthians 1, which is about God's specialty of comfort and a good many of the Psalms.

To be honest, I guess one of the things that has irritated me the most is how people avoid the subject of grief. They want to know how I am doing, but they ask someone else and not me. I don't want to do that to you, but neither do I want to cause you more pain, especially when in a public place. We try to have enough strength to say we're doing well, but sometimes, would love to be able to tear up a few phone books or something equally physical in order to vent the frustration.

I guess I am trying to say that I am here anytime you need me. I will listen, confidentially, to anything you want to say and will not try to preach to you if you need to vent. Writing my feelings was especially helpful to me, for I could confess on paper what I probably would not have done otherwise. I get impatient with myself, but am reminded by a friend that grief takes time...a long time.

I love you and pray for you often,
Joyce

Assignment for this lesson:

Practice writing kind, encouraging words in various scenarios.

1. A death in the family

2. The serious illness of a dear friend

3. A friend going through the peaks and valleys of menopause

4. Someone who has endured divorce

5. A general get well card

6. Other_____

7. Give additional reasons why letter writing may be a good solution. Write a sample letter.

6

WHY?

"*Give heed to me and answer me; I am restless in my complaint and am surely distracted,*" Psalm 55:2.

We do many things in our lives that come about because of expectation of change. When we know there's going to be a change in our lives, we prepare. When we expect a child, we study pregnancy and childbirth. We seek whatever resources are available when we have some difficulty in family life, whether it is how to file taxes, how to guide a toddler through the terrible two's or how to deal with a teenager who is losing his or her way. It helps us to understand the situation better and enables us to deal with our problems in a logical way.

When we're faced with an unexpected tragedy, it's normal to examine it; to hunt for some kind of logical explanation. When we cannot, we ask, *why?*

Frequent comments are:

Why did this happen?
For what purpose?
Is God trying to tell me something?
What is God trying to tell me?
Am I being punished? If so, for what?
What do I need to learn from this?
Why me? Well, why not me?
I can't understand it.
If only...
I can't begin to see any good purpose in this.
It makes no sense.
I just cannot give him/her up.
There are no satisfactory answers.
How can I ever be happy again?
I'll never be normal again.

It's futile to try to discover God's purpose in any certain event or if He had a purpose at all. He alone has these answers and has not revealed His thinking on these matters. Many tragedies cannot be predicted nor can most be attributed to any certain cause.

God is in control, even when it appears that He is not! Guilt begins to creep in because we asked the *why* question in the first place. It isn't shameful to ask *why*. Our first impulse is to ask *why?* Why don't we reveal our hearts to God and ask more questions instead of feeling guilty for doing so? Reading Job once more may help us to understand this better. Job had *lots* of questions. As Christians, God is with us ~ we are His children. He is our Father; our Healer; our Counselor; our Guide. He wants us to come to Him.

Dear Lord, please ~ help me figure this out. In no way do I want to discredit you, but I just don't understand it all.

Think back for a minute to Old Testament history. The Midianites were giving the Israelites all sorts of grief after they finally conquered the land of Canaan. Because of their idolatry, God allowed them to be heavily oppressed by Midian for 7 years. As soon as they would get crops up, Midian would come and destroy them. They were experts in oppression and Israel was hitting bottom on the scale of discouragement. Wouldn't you? How many of us can do without food?! Israel had taken to the hills and was living in caves in the mountains. An angel appeared to Gideon as he was beating out wheat in a wine press. He was there to keep from being discovered because food was so scarce!

The angel said, "The Lord is with you, O valiant warrior." And listen to Gideon's reply. Why?! *"O my lord, if the Lord is with us,* **why** *then has all this happened to us?"* Judges 6:12,13. Later in the same verse he cries, *"Now the Lord has abandoned us!"* Sound familiar?

Joshua also asked *why*? In Joshua 7, when conquering Canaan, just after losing the battle with Ai, Joshua tore his clothes and fell to the earth on his face before the ark of the

Lord until evening, even putting dirt on his head, a sign of deep grief. His heart was broken! He didn't know there was sin in the camp. Joshua said, *"Alas, O Lord God, why didst Thou ever bring this people over the Jordan, only to deliver us into the hand of the Amorites, to destroy us?"* Joshua 7:7.

> ## Joshua wasn't able to know all that God knew, so his response was WHY, WHY, WHY?

It just didn't make sense! Joshua wasn't able to know all that God knew, so his response was *WHY, WHY, WHY?*

Mentally picture a chart as you read the next few paragraphs. On one side, we could line up all the scriptures that tell us of God's love, mercy, compassion and care and on the other side we could list all the events that were difficult. God's plan didn't let Jeremiah escape being thrown into a dungeon or spare Joseph the pain and imprisonment he suffered, and yet Joseph was able to say, *"God meant it for good,"* Genesis 50:20.

Did God explain to Joseph what was going to happen, and how it would all fit together? *Listen, Joseph, you're going to be thrown in a pit by your brothers and sold as a slave and then you'll spend a couple of years in prison as a result of a terrible injustice, but it'll be all right! Just hang in there.* No, Joseph did not have that privilege, nor do we. God does not see time as we do. Unknown to Joseph, there was a purpose for him and fulfilling that purpose would take a great deal of time.

However, when Joseph looked back, he could tell that the things that happened had all worked for good. Joseph had a trusting heart, full of faith in God but he had to get a few miles down the road of life before he could look back and see that God meant it for good. (See a lesson in that?) We cannot conclude that God planned it that way, but we can know that God *uses* situations to create good. He used the evil in the hearts of Joseph's brothers to an advantage, to raise him as a leader.

According to Romans 8:28, "*all things work together for good, to those who love God; to those who are called according to His purpose.*" He causes things to work together ~ it didn't say He made it happen. The NIV reads, "*and we know that in all things God works for the good of those who love him....*" Whatever happens God can use our situations to further His purpose. The same God that permitted James the apostle to be killed by Herod in Acts 12, *protected* Peter and allowed him to be released from prison. We, by faith, have to accept God's workings with the knowledge that *Father knows best.*

> **We, by faith, have to accept God's workings with the knowledge that Father knows best**

When we're riddled with fresh grief, our emotions allow us to twist this, and say, *Why did God do this? Did God cause this? Why did this happen? Am I doing something wrong? Am I being punished?* As pointed out by Harold Kushner in When Bad Things Happen To Good People, our plea should not be *why did you let this happen?* but *God, you can see what's happening, please help me!*[17]

Remember the men on the road to Emmaus? They didn't even realize Jesus was walking right there beside them. They had seen him crucified three days earlier and they were confused and depressed! All their hopes were crushed. He had given them such hope and now He was gone. They could not logically line up all the evidence. When we are in the middle of stressful, painful times and cannot lighten the heaviness of loss and grief, it's sometimes hard to remember the evidence. Jesus *is* walking beside us, and He said we could "*cast all our anxiety upon Him because He cares for us,*" 1 Peter 5:7.

Which would be more comforting? To coldly quote *all things work together for good* and leave the griever to wonder how that will happen, or to say, *I'm not sure that I have the answer or that anyone else does. We cannot know how God will work this together, but surely, as time goes on, there will be some good thing that will result.*

After Jill's death, we heard of many young people who were inspired to give their lives a spiritual check up. Several were baptized. Many years previous, one couple had lost an 11 year old son to cancer. They were not Christians at the time. Wylene had since been baptized but Emory was mad at God. Someone had told him that it had happened because there was sin in his life, so for many years he blamed God. Although many had studied with Emory, he was baptized after Jill died. He thought we were good people and that God wouldn't do that to us. Good things do result.

Illness and death were brought here by Satan. We mistakenly blame God for events that were caused by sin. Evil is responsible for many tragedies but just as with Joseph, God can work it for good. Many parents spend hour after hour, which turns into days and years trying to make sense of the why question and ultimately find they have to give up that quest in order to live. How much better if they could turn their attention to God, saving the anger, hurt and stress that can be so damaging.

We tend to live our lives with relative ease, getting somewhat complacent and being comfortable with our routines. Being a fairly well organized person, I like my ducks in a row. We want them to stay in step and be predictable. We want to be in control, but one turn of events can totally change our world and upset our entire outlook on life and eternity. We would prefer life to be completely fair so that suffering can be avoided. If life were spelled out for us in such detail and such predictability, would we be people of faith? Or would we be robots? Would we want God to tell us what is going to happen in the future? You may be answering *yes* in your mind, but think carefully. Would you really? Are we forgetting that in all the fairness, there would be no grace? Grace is, after all, unmerited favor.

If we're worried about God's reactions to our questions, we can remember God was patient with Gideon as he reaffirmed his faith. Chapter six of Judges is interesting testimony as Gideon asks for a sign from God. As an angel instructed, he prepared an offering of meat and bread and placed it on a rock.

When the angel touched his staff to the offering, fire sprang up and consumed it. Gideon showed his insecurity as he asked for more signs (the wet fleece and the dry fleece ~ notice God's patience?) and then went on to lead Israel to victory after his meltdown in Midian.

Joshua, too, won many battles after experiencing life's lessons at Ai. Joseph certainly had some stories to tell after the surprises life threw at him.

Even Jesus dealt with death and illness and we can see how He reacted to grief and difficulty because of the account of Lazarus. It shows His compassion and His willingness to help His friends, and the power that was shown at that time surely strengthened their faith in Him. It didn't look like Jesus was going to respond at first and Martha was more than a little bent out of shape about it.

She met Him outside the village and said, *"Lord, if you had been here, my brother would not have died."* But her faith was strong as she said, *"Even now, I know that whatever You ask of God, God will give You."* She was pleading with him for her brother's life. He had a purpose and had deliberately stayed away in order to be glorified in a greater way ~ to instill and strengthen more faith in those who were witnesses of this event. When He told Martha her brother would rise again, she answered that she knew there was a resurrection. Mary, who had been sitting in the house, came out and poured out her feelings, repeating these same things to Jesus, falling at His feet. They were friends. These women had suffered a great loss. He loved them all and their pain and tears and the tears of those with them moved Him so deeply, Scripture tells us, *"Jesus wept,"* John 11:35.

Some time ago we were reviewing some of John Clayton's tapes. John is a converted atheist who edits the *Does God Exist?*[18] material. He pointed out that when Lazarus died, Jesus wept, not because He would never see Lazarus again, for He was soon to raise him from the dead. He was weeping for the family, for us, for all we have to go through because of sin in the world.

Tears have their own language. Mary's confidence in Jesus was surely bolstered as she saw His kindness and compassion. It should bolster our confidence as well, realizing with what depth He cares for us.

Psalm 147 begins with praise to the Lord and verse 3 says *"He heals the broken hearted and binds up their wounds."* Psalm 145 reads *"The Lord is gracious and full of compassion, slow to anger and great in mercy. The Lord is good to all, and His tender mercies are over all His works."*

Tragedy is heartbreak; sad, hard, final and disturbing. Tragedy shakes us; that's why it's called tragedy. Many lose loved ones who are not living in a way that will honor God and then become discouraged themselves as if they had control over the situation, or could have prevented it in some way. Conversation is punctuated with *why* and *what if.* Since it is usually easier to cope if death is due to illness, the harder task is comforting someone whose loved one died because of sin. With all the broken heartedness that is possible today as the result of sin, our ability to comfort those who are hurting needs to be sharpened daily. We could point out scriptures that will boost and build faith, but they may not be able to process that information at first. More importantly, we can simply state *you will survive this.* Most of us know and understand what the Bible teaches about salvation, and it is not our responsibility to decide anyone's eternal destiny. There is no set age for obedience and we can trust God to do the very best thing. They need to know that there will be better times. Scripture holds the key when we worry and obsess about things over which we have no control.

"Finally, brethren, whatever is true, whatever is honorable (noble), whatever is right (just), whatever is pure, whatever is lovely, whatever is of good repute (report), if there is any excellence and if anything worthy of praise, <u>let your mind dwell on these things</u>,"
Philippians 4:8.

Those who hang onto their faith in spite of whatever tragedy or sadness is confronting them, become stronger in the process; more able to serve God and to help others.

Nothing can be done to change the past but the past can change us, either for good or bad

Accidents come with even more baggage. What if we hadn't given him the car keys that night? Why did we give him that bicycle for his birthday? Why did we let her go to the lake? Grievers can endlessly question themselves, trying to find relief. Suicide brings waves of questions and self examination. Where did I go wrong? Why couldn't I see the signs? What were they thinking and why was I not paying attention?

Our family has been broken hearted by the effects of illness, and we know many other families have also been broken hearted by deaths caused by drunken drivers, tragic illnesses, automobile accidents, murder and suicide. Nothing can be done to change the past but the past can change us, either for good or bad. God's Word does bind up our wounds and give us hope.

Guilt and regret are poisons and spending too much time with the why question can not only hinder progress but it can hinder the development of a more intimate relationship with God. Some things in life simply do not have answers. Hanging onto guilt for whatever reason will only bring more pain, more anxiety and will possibly change relationships with other family members and with God.

Questions for study and discussion:

1. How would you respond to a Christian who is asking *why*?

2. How would you respond to a non-Christian who is asking the same question?

3. Make a chart with scriptures of hope on one side, and situations that seem hopeless on the other.

4. Discuss the difference between all things being good and working for good.

5. How did the death of Lazarus work for good?

UNFOLDING THE ROSEBUD

It is only a tiny rosebud,
A flower of GOD's design;
But I cannot unfold the petals
with these clumsy hands of mine.

The secret of unfolding flowers
Is not known to such as I.
GOD opens this flower so sweetly,
When in my hands they fade and die.

If I cannot unfold a rosebud
This flower of GOD's design,
Then how can I think I have wisdom
To unfold this life of mine?

So I'll trust in Him for His leading,
Each moment of every day.
I will look to him for His guidance,
Each step of the pilgrim way.

The pathway that lies before me,
Only my Heavenly Father knows.
I'll trust Him to unfold the moments,
Just as He unfolds the rose.

Bryan T. Burgess

It Makes Me so Mad, I Could....

"He who is slow to anger has great understanding, but he who is quick tempered exalts folly," Proverbs 14:29.

God created us all with the ability to feel emotion. Some emotional responses feel good and some do not. Whether we share a happy thought, a compassionate moment or become overly protective because of fear, all these reactions come from emotion. Many are perceived as positive; some negative. Irritation, indignation, and wrath are also emotions that can be used either positively or negatively. Most of the time, we're able to keep these emotions in reasonable control, although an occasional tear may slide down the cheek or an unkind word will slip out of our mouths. All of us are emotional; some more than others. Some may have apologies to make when emotion is not channeled in proper ways. The displaying of feelings may actually be what draws us to certain personalities. Many of us would surely be drawn to someone who displays a kind regard for the feelings of others.

Please imagine the emotions that might come as you are confronted with the following:

- Two soldiers from our U.S. armed forces arrive at your front door.

- A spouse left home to do an errand and never returned.

- A simple medical procedure was the answer to a health problem, but the look on the surgeon's face said something is very wrong.

- A young man voted most likely to succeed in college was stabbed to death on a field trip to a big city.

- A doctor stands before you with the news that your child has an incurable condition.

- I'm sorry, but testing reveals the early stages of Alzheimers.

- The phone rings and that call changes your life forever.

This page could be filled with possible scenarios, and nothing we can say or do will change the outcome of these situations. We are left to deal with the anger, despair, helplessness and fatigue that follow.

Anger may come from the feeling of injustice because of a particular offence or a feeling of helplessness because of the complexities of choosing treatments for a difficult illness or for aging parents. It may be that the anger and guilt are combined; directed at self ~ for some perceived oversight or mistake.

Having learned from two types of anger in the Bible, the <u>assertive anger</u> that will help a certain cause and the <u>irresponsible anger</u> that is motivated by sin, we as Christians are concerned about responding to anger in a way that will be healing to ourselves and helpful to others.

Anger, as it applies to grieving, can be separated into four categories:

- Anger at the perpetrator of an injustice
- Anger at the deceased
- Anger at self
- Anger at God

We can *choose* how we will respond to anger. It's to our advantage, both physically and spiritually, to respond positively.

Anger can be directed in such a way as to be profitable. John Walsh, of the popular FOX television show, *America's Most Wanted*, started that campaign because of the horrific death of his son, Adam, who was abducted and murdered. John Walsh's organization has apprehended nearly 1,000 dangerous criminals in the last 25 years. Our children are safer because of this man's productively managed anger.

Mothers Against Drunk Drivers (MADD) began in Sacramento, California in 1980 by Candace Lightner. Her thirteen year old daughter, Cari, was happily walking to a carnival with a friend, when she was killed by a drunken driver, but on probation with three prior convictions. This offense was his fifth in four years. MADD is now the largest crime victims' organization in the world; its beginning brought a little peace to distraught parents.

Scholarships and memorials can be established in honor of the deceased at medical or educational institutions, where in years to come, others will benefit.

These injustices leave us in rage; yet, at the same time feeling somewhat helpless. Our first impulse is to DO SOMETHING, ANYTHING! If anger is not dealt with properly, bitterness and revenge can develop and be very damaging. Anger channeled in the right way can be profitable, though many of us are not equipped either emotionally, physically or financially to start national organizations. Anger that is not managed will not only lead to sin, but to a life of unhappiness. Where do we put our anger when we pray?

"But I say to you, love your enemies and pray for those who persecute you in order that you may be sons of your Father who is in heaven; for He causes His sun to rise on the evil and the good, and sends rain on the righteous and the unrighteous," Matthew 5:44,45.

Compassionate Friends is a wonderful organization that provides a safe place for grieving parents to talk about their children. There are chapters to be found nationally. Our local chapter didn't seem to be the right thing for me at the time. I didn't go for several months but had spoken with a *phone friend* a couple of times. Our conversations revealed that she was still full of hate for the drunken driver that took her son's life five years previously. When I did go to a meeting, it had the same tone. Everyone sat around and spoke of their misery, so I didn't return. I know I didn't give it a fair evaluation and have heard so many good things about that organization, but that's definitely not where I wanted to be in five years. I was not expecting the grief process to take so long and was very impatient.

> **If there is a need to spend countless hours volunteering in order to cope, it can become a form of idolatry**

For Christians, as good as these organizations are, there is a danger of becoming overly involved in order to cope with grief. If there is a need to spend countless hours volunteering in order to cope, it can become a form of idolatry. Don't misunderstand, there are many worthy organizations desperate for volunteer help and being able to help is very satisfying. If hours donated take away from our family and from our walk with God, it can become idolatry. God hasn't changed his policy on idolatry. He didn't like it when Israel practiced it and He still wants our attention now. Remember too, as you read on, that we can also make idols out of hatred, bitterness, revenge and self-pity by holding onto them, rather than giving them up.

Some anger may be directed at the deceased, especially if his or her death is sudden. A spouse may feel deserted and overwhelmed with the details of daily living. There's no one with whom to converse about bill paying, investments, upkeep of property and so on. *Why did you have to die and leave me with this mess* is a common thought pattern.

If the death is from suicide, it actually helps to be able to blame the deceased. Guilt that surrounds this situation can be unbearable and the grieving family usually suffers alone because there is so much shame involved and friends feel powerless, not realizing they can help just by being there. Parents or spouses think they should have recognized the signs or been able to intervene in some way, blaming themselves.

Typical questions are: *Where did I go wrong? Why couldn't I see the signs? Was I not paying attention?* Actually, the questions should be: *Where did the child or spouse go wrong? What were they thinking?* The one who took his or her own life made the decision. The decision may have been warped by drug abuse, medication or a troubled mind but it was still the decision of the deceased and it helps some families to be able to consign blame. It relieves guilt, especially for siblings.

Blaming self is usually because of some perceived guilt. Sudden infant death syndrome, for which there is no visible cause, brings extreme anguish to parents. Endless questions don't bring any answers. Other parents will question their decision-making as discussed in the previous chapter. We realize the dilemma of parents when they try to place blame somewhere ~ anywhere, in order to have relief from their pain. Support groups or professional counseling by a qualified Christian counselor may be an option for some, in order to help them realize they had no part in bringing about their child's death.

> Extreme care must be taken when comforting, so as not to make statements that will place blame

Extreme care must be taken when comforting, so as not to make statements that will place blame. Some will blame God and some Christians have little understanding of the need to express anger in the early stages of grief. The following is an excerpt from <u>On Grief and Grieving: Finding the Meaning of Grief Through the Five Stages of Loss</u>, by Elizabeth Kubler-Ross, M.D. and David Kessler.

"When Heather's teenage daughter died at sixteen, Heather was furious at God for allowing her to die so young, with a life so unlived. Heather's family was deeply involved in the church that had been a strong support during her daughter's illnesses, but they had difficulty dealing with Heather's anger. She no longer wanted to hear about the God who answers prayers, since her prayers had not been answered. She felt judged by her friends at church for having so much anger at God. A friend said to her cautiously, *be careful not to evoke the wrath of God.*

At that, Heather was even more enraged. *What is He going to do, she retorted, take my daughter away? What's he going to do, take me? That would be fine. I'd rather be with her than be here.* Her friend knelt down and said tenderly, *let's pray for forgiveness.* At that moment, Heather decided to leave behind her church and a number of friends. It was years before she walked back into the church.

If we ask people to move through their anger too fast, we only alienate them. Whenever we ask people to be different than they are, or to feel something different, we are not accepting them as they are and where they are. Nobody likes to be asked to change and not be accepted as they are. We like it even less in the midst of grief." [19]

Although change is needed and must come about, we can again see the wisdom of remaining silent and letting the grievers express themselves without casting judgment, realizing that their outlook may be changed in a very short time. If we wait patiently, building trust and support, time will present the right opportunity to re-establish or strengthen faith in God.

How can the point of peace be reached? The wound from such a loss is deep but if the wound cannot be healed because of anger and bitterness, what has been gained? It would be shameful for the loss to destroy yet another life.

Ephesians 4, in giving instructions for the new Christian life, tells us to put on a new self, which is in the likeness of God. The first admonition is to speak the truth, and the next is, "*Be angry, and yet do not sin; do not let the sun go down on your anger and do not give the devil an opportunity,*" Ephesians 4:26, 27. In other words, don't <u>stay</u> angry.

Jesus certainly became angry. The most common mention

is when he turned over the tables of the moneychangers in the temple (Matthew 21:12), and He had some choice words for the scribes and Pharisees in Matthew 23, calling them whitewashed tombs, among other things! We all know where our weak points lie, and some have to work harder to bring those weak traits under control.

Abundant resources are available to help move through the grief process. I have a ton of grief books, and each has at least a thought or two that has been helpful, but lasting, true relief will come from God's Word. That relief can only come by knowing it and the more that is learned, the more we appreciate it.

Psalm 37:7-9 reads, *"Rest in the Lord and wait patiently for Him; do not fret because of him who prospers in his way, because of the man who carries out wicked schemes. Cease from anger, and forsake wrath; Do not fret, it leads only to evildoing. For evildoers will be cut off, but those who wait for the Lord, they will inherit the land."*

> **I have a ton of grief books, and each has at least a thought or two that has been helpful, but lasting, true relief will come from God's Word**

Key words: Rest and wait. I try to remember that. In the early years, I wondered often how a perfectly healthy young woman could develop a brain tumor. It was one of the questions being saved for heaven. Now, I realize that when I am so privileged to be in God's presence, it will no longer be important.

Anger will not be such a problem if we work hard to grow in other areas: love, joy, compassion, concern, and gentleness. James tells us to be *"quick to hear, slow to speak and slow to anger; for the anger of man does not achieve the righteousness of God,"* James 1:19-20. When giving instructions for the new life, Ephesians 4 continues in verse 31, *"Let all bitterness and wrath and anger and clamor and slander be put away from you, along with all malice."*

"He who is slow to anger is better than the mighty and he who rules his spirit, than he who captures a city,"

Proverbs 16:32

Questions for study and discussion:

1. Discuss the difference between assertive anger and aggressive anger.

2. Give some examples of assertive anger and the good it can produce.

3. Discuss the emotions, both good and bad that may be produced by grief counseling.

4. What are some situations that are most likely to produce anger?

5. Discuss solutions to anger.

For further study: Consult works on anger by Les Carter. His book <u>Good 'N Angry</u>, used as a source for this chapter, is now out of print. Several different titles dealing with anger are now available.

Grief is like a River

By Cinthia G. Kelley

My grief is like a river,
I have to let it flow,
But I myself determine
Just where the banks will go.

Some days the current takes me
In waves of guilt and pain
But there are always quiet pools
Where I can rest again.

I crash on rocks of anger;
My faith seems faint indeed,
But there are other swimmers
Who know that what I need

Are loving hands to hold me
When waters are too swift,
But someone kind to listen
When I just seem to drift.

Grief's river is a process
If relinquishing the past
By swimming in hope's channels
I'll reach the shore at last.

I Can Wait...If it Doesn't Take too Long

"Like a city that is broken into and without walls is a man who has no control over his spirit," Proverbs 25:28.

We, as Americans, just don't like to wait ~ we'd rather do anything but wait. After all, we have microwaves, cell phones, instant banking, ATM'S, credit cards and easy pay. We kind of like having things available on demand. Anyone who has sent a son or daughter out on the first date knows the agony of waiting until he or she arrives safely home. How many times did you look out the window?? Or at your watch??

We've developed our own systems for waiting while in line at the bank, at the grocery, and while traffic is stalled on the freeway. (It's a great time to pray!) But waiting for grief to fade is a different challenge. Paul said he had *learned to be content* in his circumstances, Philippians 4:11. He developed it; it didn't come naturally for him and it doesn't come naturally for us.

After all the details of the funeral and burial are attended to, the sadness lingers and desire to return to normal life slowly returns. The desire may be there but fulfilling it may be more difficult. After my brother's wife died, he said if it weren't for his children, he'd just sign on to a fishing boat and wait for a year to go by. He knew his children would need to see him and to know he was progressing in his adjustment. Please realize that first year has lots of hurdles. Some memories may fade temporarily but when holidays and special days come around, the grief will resurface. These times together, while enjoyable, can also be very painful. There's always that reminder at family gatherings of one who isn't there. Grief can be lived through and learned from, but it is not something we can *get over*. There is a strong desire to be able to spend one day without being reminded and to have a sense of normalcy again, but there is no choice but to wait.

Self-control is one of the fruits of the spirit in Galatians 5, and 2 Peter 1:6 says to add self-control to other virtues. Pity the child who has been raised without it and we've probably all been around someone who needs more of it! Our youngest son has two precious daughters who are being home schooled. (Yes, I'm going to brag about my grandchildren!) They both were taught at an early age to express themselves without whining and as a result, they have large vocabularies. When one of them would get in a *mood,* she would be told to go to a specific place and fold her hands until she could gain a little self-control. It has proven very effective and it has been my thinking that we need to impose this rule on a few adults! The ten-year-old sets her alarm for 7 a.m. so she can get up and watch one of her sessions of video school before breakfast. Even though she may not realize it, her self-control habits are already being established.

> **Self-control is vital if we're going to bring glory to the name of God**

Waiting and self-control are hard to master. Minds, thoughts and actions have to be guarded, especially when weak with distraction and frustration. At this point we may be longing for the peace of God which surpasses all comprehension. Because of frustration, fuzzy thinking will take its toll, but self-control will help us out of those ruts and allow us to move to more productive thinking.

The first rule of thumb when computers get cranky is to reboot. Sometimes the problem will cure itself. We may just have to hit our own personal restart button when we get into a pity party or a trend of negative thinking. While we can be frustrated and anxious without sin, these things can lead to sin. Self-control is vital if we're going to bring glory to the name of God.

Most of us have no problem being able to deal with life as long as it makes sense. Many things in life have a logical pattern. If we do a certain thing, other things are sure to follow. We still like having those *ducks in a row.* I don't believe this is uniquely a problem for women, but it does seem we have a little more difficulty with it than most men.

My mom is the example that comes to mind. She always had a tiger in her tank. She was 90 at the time of her death in February, 2006 and fortunately, ill health only came to her a few months before she died. Up until that time, she still had that tiger, and would quickly tell you that she wanted to be driving her own car when she reached 100. If she was faced with a situation, she did whatever was needed to solve it and put that behind her. Her motto: *If you don't know how to do it ~ learn!* She, of necessity, worked outside the home until her retirement. This same spirit allowed her to learn how to swim and to teach her first ladies Bible class at age 70. She taught her last at age 89.

Five years earlier, my dad preceded her in death at age 88. It was with great difficulty that my mom dealt with his unstable health and failing memory. She couldn't predict what was coming next and she didn't like it. Daddy was part of the problem but the other part was her inability to take each day as it came. Waiting for the unknown is difficult, as anyone who has waited for medical test results can testify. Can you remember a personal trial that was particularly difficult? It may be compounded when age is a factor and death may be just around the corner. Fortunately, she faced his death with the same determination with which she faced life. Facing her own failing health, unable to predict what was coming next, was not to her liking either but she didn't lose her determination. And once again, even in her health care, lessons were learned about taking each day as it comes.

> *"...do not be anxious for your life, as to what you shall eat, or what you shall drink; nor for your body, as to what you shall put on. Is not life more than food, and the body than clothing? Look at the birds of the air, that they do not sow, neither do they reap, nor gather into barns, and yet your heavenly Father feeds them. Are you not worth much more than they?"*
> Matthew 6:25, 26.

Saul had a self-control problem. In 1 Samuel 15, he was supposed to completely destroy everything concerning the Amalekites. Unfortunately, he had not been in the habit of being self-controlled, so he, against God's will, saved things that looked good to him and suffered the consequences.

Practicing controlled thinking and counting blessings will keep grief from increasing. The circumstances of our lives cannot be controlled, but we can control how we respond. Because of distraction, fuzzy thinking will take its toll, but scripture, along with waiting and self-control will help normalize thinking. While vulnerable, we need to be praying that we won't do anything stupid. Life-changing decisions should be avoided during this time.

"Like a city that is broken into and without walls is a man who has no control over his spirit," Proverbs 25:28.

> David was a deeply spiritual man and while he praised God continually in the Psalms, he also poured out his agonies to God

".....taking every thought captive to the obedience of Christ," 2 Corinthians 10:5.

Points for grievers to remember:

1. **Those around you are *trying* to help**. Help them to help you ~ they can't read your mind.

2. **Don't be defensive**. People mean well, even if they may not say *just the right thing*. Give them a break. Live and behave in such a way as to bring honor to God. Do I mean your hurt and agony should be put aside just to present a front to others? No. But we need to deal with others with patience and kindness even if we don't feel like it.

3. **Recognize your thinking may be faulty**. Wait it out.

Read. Pray. Did you ever wonder how David addressed God as he did in the Psalms? David was a deeply spiritual man and while he praised God continually in the Psalms, he also poured out his agonies to God. Spend time with the Psalms of David and let his depth and strength be an example and encouragement in gaining more of your own.

> Scripture has a calming influence and can lead us in our desperate attempts to find peace

4. **Admit you may be angry**. Direct the anger properly. It's not uncommon to be angry with the one you lost or the one who is ill. Perhaps you're angry at someone else. It's common to want to blame someone! Anyone! It's not a sin to be angry, but it is a sin to remain that way. Find a way to channel the anger. Even though we had no reason to blame one another, Frank and I were acutely aware of the divorce rate of parents who had lost a child. Each one may think their grief is greater or one may think the other somehow failed in a responsibility. Even if there was a fault that caused the death, placing blame does not heal or bring back the beloved. Scripture has a calming influence and can lead us in our desperate attempts to find peace.

Take out the aggression somehow. Find a friend and tear up a few phone books together! My standing joke with a friend in Lakeland, who has been through an incredible amount of difficulty and an ugly divorce was, *when will we find time to tear up a few phone books!* Do something therapeutic! Go to the gym. Find a hobby. Take a class. Study what the Bible says about the subject of anger.

5. **You may need to change some habits**. ER may no longer be your favorite TV program, especially if you've spent much time there! Change some music. Rod Stewart's version of *Have I told you lately that I love you* had a particular memory for Jill, and every time I hear it, I am reminded. A friend's dad had recorded that song for his wife on a special occasion. The tape was on her breakfast tray as she was served breakfast in bed and what 19 year old girl would not be impressed with

hat romantic display of affection! It's frequently played on the radio stations I listen to, so I have just learned to smile and enjoy it. If a particular thing makes you crumble, try to avoid it for a while, until you're stronger.

6. **Get out of the house**. Don't stay isolated. After that teary spell, comb your hair or put on some fresh makeup and leave the house, even if it is just to take a walk. Notice things around you. Appreciate the trees and flowers and learn to give thanks for anything of God's beauty. A house being built means someone is anticipating new surroundings. Give thanks. Try not to refuse invitations from friends if at all possible. Self pity is *not* attractive.

7. **Develop an awareness and take precautions against negative thinking**. Look at the end result. Where will that thinking bring us? Is it profitable? If anger, hopelessness and frustration seem to be too prominent, change courses. Ask God to calm your spirit and begin to look around you for good things that will substitute for negative thinking; things that will help you find and enjoy God's presence. In turn, this new action will bring glory to God.

8. **Research things that brought joy to Bible people**. Read related materials. Invest in some books of inspirational humor and cartoons, inspiring stories, or try writing your own uplifting material and sharing it with others. We truly have to *exercise* ourselves to godliness. What happened the last time you started an exercise program? Those sore muscles are testimony to the fact that exercising is work! So if you are the griever, get started ~ or determine to help a grieving friend.

Questions for study and discussion:

1. List the most difficult times when grieving.

2. Discuss ways to develop self-control.

3. Why is prolonged anxiety wrong?

4. Discuss proper attitudes toward those who are trying to help.

5. Brainstorm things grievers can do to help themselves.

"The Lord is good to those who wait for Him, to the person who seeks Him," Lamentations 3:25.

Wait

Psalm 37:4
By Russell Kelfer

Desperately, helplessly, longingly, I cried.
Quietly, patiently, lovingly, God replied.
I pled and wept for a clue to my fate,
And the Master so gently said, "Child, you must wait."

"Wait? You say, wait?" my indignant reply.
"Lord, I need answers, I need to know why!
Is Your hand shortened? Or have you not heard?
By faith I have asked, and am claiming Your word."

"My future and all to which I can relate
Hangs in the balance, and You tell me to wait?
I'm needing a 'yes,' a go-ahead sign,

Or even a 'no' to which I can resign.
And Lord, I've been asking, and this is my cry:
I'm weary of asking! I need a reply!"

Then quietly, softly, I learned of my fate
As my Master replied once again, "You must wait."
So, I slumped in my chair, defeated and taut
And grumbled to God, "So, I'm waiting...for what?"
He seemed then, to kneel, and His eyes met with mine,
And He tenderly said, "I could give you a sign. I could
shake the heavens and darken the sun.
I could raise the dead, and cause mountains to run.
All you seek, I could give, and pleased you would be.
You would have what you want ~ but you wouldn't know Me.

You'd not know the depth of My love for each saint:
You'd not know the power that I give to the faint;
You'd not learn to see through clouds of despair;
You'd not learn to trust just by knowing I'm there;
You'd not know the joy of resting in Me
When darkness and silence were all you could see.
You'd never experience that fullness of love
As the peace of My spirit descends like a dove;
You'd know that I give and I save...(for a start)
But you'd know the depth of the beat of my heart.

The glow of My comfort late into the night,
The faith that I give when you walk without sight,
The depth that's beyond getting just what you asked,
Of an infinite God, who makes what you have last.

You'd never know, should your pain quickly flee,
What it means that "My grace is sufficient for thee."
"Yes your dreams for your loved one overnight
would come true,
but, oh, the loss! If I lost what I'm doing in you!

So, be silent, my child, and in time you will see
That the greatest of gifts is to get to know ME.
And though oft' may My answer seem terribly late,
My most precious answer of all is still "WAIT." [20]

9

New Lives and Customs

"The Lord will command His loving kindness in the daytime; and His song will be with me in the night, a prayer to the God of my life," Psalm 42:8

In the closing scenes of the movie <u>Castaway</u>,[21] Chuck Nolan, the main character played by Tom Hanks, is telling a friend of his three year ordeal on a deserted island after having survived a plane crash. Chuck was the type of guy who needed to be in control of everything, so his island experience was very revealing. At one point, he was in the depths of despair and had entertained the idea of suicide but his simple plan to end his life didn't work.

He continues, *that's when this feeling came over me like a warm blanket. I knew somehow that I had to stay alive ~ somehow. I had to keep breathing even though there was no reason to hope and all my logic said that I would never see this place again so that's what I did. I stayed alive and kept breathing and one day that logic was proven all wrong because the tide came in and gave me a sail and now here I am. I'm back in Memphis talking to you.* He commiserates about losing his girl friend and then says, *I know what I have to do now and I keep breathing because tomorrow the sun will rise. Who knows what the tide could bring?*

The power to live the life we want rests in our own hands. Anyone who is a parent knows unpredictable change is around every corner! Whether or not we can adapt to the change *after* trauma depends largely on how well we had direction *before* the trauma. Trauma may even bring us hidden blessings.

How do you re-enter life after some major trauma? How do you redirect your focus and manage to survive, when all you want to do is hide?

Keep breathing and get out of bed in the morning. You may think that is an over simplification, but for many, it's not an easy task. Each task that used to be performed by habit, now requires great effort. Sleep may have come, or you may have been awake most of the night. Reading is difficult because of lack of concentration. Television is senseless and watching anything related to tragedy is impossible, especially the evening news. (Those Hallmark commercials during the holidays are murder!) Even conversations with friends can only hold your attention a short while. Fatigue invades every hour.

How do you redirect your focus and manage to survive, when all you want to do is hide?

Even though our lives were turned upside down, our situation didn't require any devastating life changes. Frank and I still had each other; he still had the same job, we lived in the same place, had the same friends ~ just no Jill. Our three sons were all in Alabama with their own lives to live. Life for us would continue on. She was the youngest of our four children and even though she had been away at school, there was an abrupt silence in our home ~ no more kids home for the weekend; no extra meals to cook. We even considered moving from our house to another, but where could we go to escape memories? I couldn't even go to the grocery without wanting to buy Pop-Tarts and Jolly Ranchers. Reminders were everywhere!

We tried to be normal; to keep the same routine and be involved in our usual activities. Since grief brings about a certain amount of solitude, we had to work at our relationship; being sure not to shut one another out. Fortunately, we had no one to blame. Blame serves no good purpose anyway. She didn't die at the hands of someone's carelessness; no medical intervention could have helped her and there was no one to whom we could direct anger; no *what if* or *if only*.

Just a few days previously, we each had stated our love for one another; Frank talked to Jill just before he left for Romania, and I spoke to her in a phone conversation the day before her collapse. Later on, I learned to count this as a blessing as anger is destructive and lack of forgiveness will rot away your very being. What if our last words had been a quarrel? It would have been much more difficult had we just had an argument or if there were unfinished emotional business. Regret can be bitter.

Divorce or the death of a spouse may bring about a totally different lifestyle and necessary changes will be made. Divorce may actually be more devastating, because the spouse still remains and there are issues that need attention. Children may be involved and each spouse may distrust the other. Visitation may be a problem. All these details have to be worked out, in order to once again establish order, not to mention the complications if one or the other has the scriptural right to date and marry again.

For the caretaker spouse, the burden is now lifted but all the free time may be confusing until new directions can be sought. A whole new life style may be ahead.

A widow who is suddenly alone finds that financial decisions may be complicated and doing them alone is a challenge. Sleep is elusive and daily chores don't wait. With all the available talent in our church families, the appropriate help can be offered to lighten the load. One newly widowed woman rarely drove and didn't know how to pump gas! Men at church helped her with car care and taught her needed skills at the pump. The possibilities for being able to help are endless; we have to train ourselves to look for opportunities and to put aside our nervous reluctance in order to help a grieving person. Asking them to do you a favor may just provide some needed distraction. And grievers ~ they cannot read our minds and automatically know our needs! We may have to ask for that help. At times, genuine offers are made and refused because we want to be self-sufficient, only increasing the strain. Allowing others to help may be foreign to us, and saying yes will take practice.

Those suffering a miscarriage or stillbirth will put away baby items until they can be used or given to those who need them. The necessary care of older children can help distract the pain, but for those who had pinned their hopes on growing as a family, hope has been dashed, leaving loneliness and profound sadness. One couple suffered not one, but two full term stillbirths. I'm sure they stood by that baby bed many times as they dreamed and planned for the due date. The expectations now have to be put into the proper place in order to continue with life. The choice is individual, but it is not inappropriate to name the baby and have a funeral or a memorial. It serves a useful purpose in the grief process.

Remember, there are no formal rules for grieving. Unless there is a moral reason or some violation of God's will that needs to be addressed, we can help by saving our opinions ~ do not offer them unless asked. How can we all make the same decisions when we're all so individual? Spouses who have been left alone may marry again and experience happiness beyond any they could have imagined. Men are less equipped to live alone than are women, but woe to the man who decides to remarry in less than a year! The opinions start flying! Our opinions, which sometimes border on gossip, can bring even more stress to those who are grieving.

Those who have been recovering from life threatening illness will put away items related to that illness so they can return to their regular lifestyle. Their caretaking spouses have to return to their husband or wife role instead of the role of caretaker. The former patient may take an exercise class or enter some daily routine that will help them continue with a healthier lifestyle. This may be the time to branch out, try something new and redefine self so as not to be associated with illness. The climb back to a healthy life may be long and vigorous but the experience has been a convincing teacher. As health permits, attention can be given to others who may be ill, or those who are grieving. Sometimes the strength to do so has to be developed; being a comforter is not easy work! Several years ago, one of our families at church received the news no parent wants to hear. Just after New Years, their son was killed in an automobile accident and the news was delivered by a state trooper. When a friend called us, we immediately dropped everything to be with them. Yes, it was hard, even wrenching.

Are we to be comforters only when it is convenient? Not only does a new life and routine have to be established, but because of our own experiences, we can now help others whenever we have the opportunity.

During our initial grief, Frank would bury himself in work at the office, and I was left at home. Jill's room was like a magnet that drew me. Realizing we'd have to change it or I'd never be able to stay in that house, we painted the walls and chose new bed linens, and it helped, although it was still *Jill's room* until the day we moved away. Some days I would just go to the mall and walk for a while; other days would be spent in the resource room at the church building. Most people realize the need to be a working part of society, but except for some years spent working to cover college expenses for our children, my part of society was my home! There were days when I could not emotionally attend a Bible study class at church. The church where we worshipped traditionally had class before the worship hour and many times I would go into the resource room and quietly work there for that class period. There were some who did not understand. I still wanted to serve my Lord, but being with people was such a strain! Concentration was difficult and very little seemed to make sense. (Do our brains just go on vacation?) Another friend told me that after the death of her son, she cried during worship services for over a year. Imagine the strain of having a miscarriage or stillborn baby and returning to worship where there are other babies and small children. Worship is emotional ~ or at least it should be ~ and as we're trying to conquer certain emotions, worship can bring them to the surface.

Friends were kind and attentive, but when asked, *how are you?* as we tend to do by habit, I couldn't think of a satisfactory answer. I was not *fine* and could not say I was. Did they really want to hear how I had struggled that week just to be there? I'm trying to train myself to *not* ask that question to someone with fresh grief. It is such a habit, that sometimes I've said it without realizing. What's that old saying about engaging the brain before opening the mouth? When asked, you feel duty bound to tell the truth and sometimes that's really difficult! It may be one of those really bad days. There are other ways of howing interest:

- *It's good to see you!*
- *Are you able to rest at night?*
- *Do you feel you are making a reasonable adjustment?*
- *You really look nice today.*

There are trigger reactions that can not be predicted. Quite some time later, one of our sons was leading the song service and all of a sudden the tears came. He thought to himself, *now where did that come from?* It will sneak up and surprise you and tears do appear at inopportune times.

There's a cute little story by Shel Silverstein entitled <u>The missing piece</u>.[22] It's about a circle that was missing a piece, so it went about searching and as it rolled, it sang this song. *Oh, I'm lookin' for my missin' piece, I'm lookin' for my missin' piece. Hi-dee-ho, here I go, Lookin' for my missin' piece.*

It rolled through all kinds of weather and found many different pieces, but they didn't fit, so the circle continued its search. It thought happiness would only return if the piece was found, but during the search it would stop to talk to a worm or to smell a flower. Then one day, it found the perfect piece! It rolled away with a new happiness, soon realizing that it could roll very fast with this new piece; too fast to talk to the worms or smell the flowers. So it gently put down the new piece and rolled away.

All who are grieving are hoping to find their missing piece; the one that will make them whole again.

Women usually have one or two kindred spirits to whom they can turn in times of difficulty. Many times, men are the ones with the largest burden, because society seems to say that men are not supposed to grieve. Depending on occupation and finances, they may have to return to work immediately, needing to face the world bravely, putting on their happy face and pretending that nothing is wrong. When do they get to grieve? Not too long ago, our son Byron, had an opportunity to counsel his good friend and buddy whose brother had just died. He wisely e-mailed his thoughts, so it could be read in private. With permission, here are his words:

1. It will get better. After my sister died I was depressed for a very long time. I had always been able to work my way out of feeling down but couldn't this time. I finally had to go on medication for a while to get out of my cloud. But with time, it got better and the good memories are stronger than the feeling of loss.

2. You will not forget! I had a feeling that I would forget my sister and this haunted me. It was silly really ~ I think I thought of her even more. Silly little things will bring your brother to mind immediately and you'll find yourself talking at holidays and other family times about all the funny things you remember and it's always like it happened yesterday.

3. Even your body will remember when your mind forgets. Every year, around the middle of September, I seem to drag. A couple of years, I even wondered what was wrong with me. Then I was reminded that it was the day before Jill died. It's a very weird thing. I call it my annual bad day.

4. There will be bad days. Especially this first year. Every special day or event is the first one since.... It's O.K. Really. It will be better/different next year.

5. God didn't do this. You know this already I'm sure. God didn't cause any of this to happen but God can make something good out of this. You'll never know what. My sister impacted so many lives that it was amazing to me how her memory turns up when I meet people who knew her. Many have told me how her positive outlook and life and then sudden death made them think about more important things. I'm sure the same is true of your brother.

6. You're not alone. This might be the most important. Hang in there and don't isolate yourself. I did some of that and it really hurt me in the long run. I wish you had been around then to get me out on the lake or something. Time for some geo-caching?

Byron

No sermons, no *snap out of it!* But quiet trust between friends. If they're not embarrassed or afraid of tears or sadness, men have an incredible ability to counsel one another.

Not quite a year had passed when I noticed an advertisement for a grief support group sponsored by Hospice and decided to go. I did not ask Frank to go but had told him of my plans, and the night before the first meeting, he said he wanted to go too. Throughout the six weeks, there were various assignments for us to accomplish that would weave us through the grief process. The first assignment was to bring in pictures of your loved one. Since Frank had been busy that week, I chose the pictures for him to take to the next meeting. Innocently, I had interfered with what that task was to accomplish. Going through the pictures and the memories they bring was part of the recovery process. Funny, what brings comfort or joy to one person, may bring pain to another but since I was organizing a scrapbook, some of my time

> Funny, what brings comfort or joy to one person, may bring pain to another....

had already been spent remembering through pictures. I didn't recognize the importance of the task.

One of the next assignments was to make a poster that depicted the way things were, the way they are now, and the way they will be in the future; forcing us to think through the process. I had already designed my poster in my mind; not a difficult task since women frequently illustrate with pictures and posters for children's classes at church. Men don't generally do that, so it was particularly difficult for Frank. He would awaken at night in agony, torn apart by the thoughts of making that poster.

The *way things were* portion of his finished product was a picture of the three of us. (Remember, our boys had been gone for several years and Jill was the caboose.) Looking through magazines, he came up with a picture of a beautiful cake with a piece missing, to depict what *life was at the time.*

For what *life would become*, there was a picture of the two of us and a cookie with a bite missing, indicating that we would always have a missing piece. At the meeting, each participant had to explain what their poster represented. As he explained what life would become, he pointed out that we still had each other ~ just with a missing piece. The exercise of mentally thinking through the past, present and future is beneficial. There's hope at the end. The first two sessions were particularly difficult, but as time passed, it became easier. By the end of the series, the participants were laughing and joking and enjoying their time together.

> ## I felt like I'd been broken into lots of little pieces and even if all the pieces were found and glued together, the cracks would always show

What? You too? I thought I was the only one.   C.S. Lewis

Life just handed the griever a bag full of puzzle pieces; no box or instructions ~ just a bag of pieces. Establishing a life after trauma is a puzzle with no picture for a guide. Even though many have been through the same trauma and have put together their puzzle, each griever is new and has to do his own work. Some may guide and some may make suggestions, but the work is the griever's alone. Some delay putting this puzzle together, being afraid of what they will see. I told Frank that I felt like I'd been broken into lots of little pieces and even if all the pieces were found and glued together, the cracks would always show.

Scripture, meditation and prayer help the pieces to fit properly. Slowly, it comes together and there may be a few pieces missing that may not be in place for a long time, but when the picture is finally completed, it has a beauty all its own. It's not at all what you expected and is not the picture of your previous life, but lying before you is a beautiful piece of art. God is the artist, and only He knew what picture would be revealed and only He can see the greater picture.

Looking back, I now know I would have been much better

ff, had I listened to the scripture that says *"be still and know that I am God,"* Psalm 46:10 NKJV. I wanted to stay busy so I wouldn't have to think about it and that's not possible. Staying too busy delays our healing and wears us out physically. Most of our schedules are too busy anyway and we need to focus on things that will bring peace instead of frustration until we can resume a regular routine.

Focusing on the Word will simplify our lives and the benefits will go a long way in times of grief, illness and stress. My resource room visits brought focus and calm to my spare hours. Our congregation had started a new teaching program two years previously, and my commitment to work on that project for three years had already been made. A lot of hours were spent there during the first year after Jill's death and I was happy to have direction ~ something to occupy my mind. As I was organizing and providing material for our teachers, I was learning more about Bible history and it opened up a whole new area of interest for me. Our tendency in organized Bible classes is to study up to the divided kingdom and then go on to easier sections, but there are so many valuable lessons to be found in the prophets!

We know that the new life takes time and we usually mention that often to the newly grieved. It's a true statement ~ although we get really tired of hearing it. *I'm sorry that it takes so much time to heal. It will be better in time.*

It's really not the time that heals ~ it's what we DO with the time. Being patient with ourselves while we're healing will help bring calm and focus as we enter a new phase of life.

Questions for study and discussion:

1. Discuss 1 Peter 5:6-11.
   a. How can we humble ourselves?

   b. How do we cast our care upon Him?

   c. How can we invite the devil to devour?

   d. How can we conquer Satan's advances?

2. List some tragedies that require drastic changes in life.

3. How can these tragedies be used for good?

4. List six things the griever should remember.

5. What are the greatest sources for overcoming grief?

10

Rebuilding the Bridge of Faith

"And the Apostles said to the Lord, 'Increase our faith,'" Luke 17:5.

Trauma, regardless of the source, can shake us to the point that we have two choices: to either confirm wherein our faith lies or begin to question and blame God. Our prayers of faith have always risen from a deep trust in our Lord but all of a sudden, that trust seems shaky and looks strangely fragile.

Throughout our Christian lives, we build faith but when trials come, it's normal to be filled with questions. Trials may bring up questions that we've either thought of very little or have never grappled with before. Few of us are such diligent students of the Bible that we comprehend all of God's workings, plus it's not possible to know the complete mind of God. A temporary lapse of faith does not suggest denial, but a need for strengthening; a realization of weakness in self that needs to be addressed. Will faith eliminate emotional struggle? Avoid conflict? Of course not.

"If you faint in the day of adversity, your strength is small," Proverbs 24:10, NKJV.

When our loved ones are snatched from us, when our homes are robbed, vandalized or destroyed, when children are disobedient, when error grips the Church, when our nation's morals have gone by the wayside, when we feel that we are all alone because of illness, divorce or depression, we can take comfort in David's plea in Psalm 22:11 as he cries to God, *"Be not far from me, for trouble is near; for there is none to help."*

We used to live in hurricane territory and now we've traded that for tornadoes. Either way, we learned that preparations need to be made when a storm is expected. If it looks like it will cross our path, we're busy taping the windows, stocking up on canned foods, buying bottled water, lamp oil, batteries or candles, and making sure the house is secure. If needed, we evacuate to a place of safety.

The time to prepare is not when the storm hits

The time to prepare is *not* when the storm hits. By then, it's too late. If adequate preparation has not been made, we may find ourselves going haywire; agonizing at the last minute to find protection. There needs to be a plan established.

Psalm 46 begins: *"God is our refuge and strength; a very present help in trouble. Therefore we will not fear, though the earth should change, and though the mountains slip into the heart of the sea; though its waters roar and foam, though the mountains quake at its swelling pride."*

That verse actually makes me think of the devastating 2004 tsunami. Perhaps you're reading this having been survivor of nature's wrath but I doubt many of us have been tested to the point of those in the tsunami and hurricane Katrina. It's hard to conceive of every familiar thing being stripped from us but if it did happen, what would be our reaction? Our minds can still visualize the scene, as survivors of the hurricane clung to their rooftops and even treetops awaiting rescue. They were alive and they had hope. What else matters?

Visualize crawling up in God's lap and being comforted there until the storm is over

Where do we go when we hurt? If a child we go to a parent; if an adult, to a spouse or trusted friend. Visualize crawling up in God's lap and being comforted there until the storm is over; until there is time to sort out all the emotions that come with trauma. Faith is not something that just appears; it's a mental process and even though our thoughts are unstable during a crisis, we still *have an anchor that keeps our soul steadfast and sure while the billows roll.* We love that familiar hymn and sang it at Jill's funeral. Hearing others sing it too helped to strengthen us and remind us of our source of strength. Having an anchor brings hope. When trials come to shake our faith, we will not drift. We go back to what is familiar and begin again to build; re-establish our footing and secure ourselves with the promises of God and remember how they fit into our lives. Our traditional funeral services begin the process of helping us to accomplish that.

"My soul weeps because of grief; Strengthen me according to Thy word," Psalm 119: 28.

Somehow, we have come to believe that we should not have to suffer any of life's difficulties. When trials come, we cry *why me?* totally overlooking all the examples of suffering in Scripture. The heroes of faith in Hebrews 11 were not called heroes because they were born with that proverbial silver spoon in their mouths and enjoyed the best of times. They lived in a worthy way, even though they were experiencing exceedingly difficult trials.

Just studying the life of Paul should remind us that Christians do not have some sort of magical escape hatch when it comes to suffering

If we're not grounded in our faith, anxiety and despair can creep in to consume our thoughts to the point of sin. Just studying the life of Paul should remind us that Christians do not have some sort of magical escape hatch when it comes to suffering. Paul had confidence that God would deliver him and he knew the value of asking others to pray for him, Romans 15:30. We're sometimes embarrassed to ask for the prayers of others. Why, I wonder? Do we associate that with weakness? Actually, it's a sign of strength to recognize what Paul recognized; that God answers prayer and that joy comes from being with and praying with others. He found *refreshing rest* in their company, Romans 15:32, 33. But, that's another chapter.

In A Case for Faith by Lee Stroebel, Lee, an atheist, is

interviewing Peter Kreeft, PhD., a religious educator, author and philosopher with a long list of credits. Lee is on a quest to discredit Christianity and while doing so, becomes a believer. Lee and Kreeft are discussing the problem of human suffering ~ a subject that weakens the faith of many.

Kreeft: "God's answer to the problem of suffering is that he came right down into it. Many Christians try to get God off the hook for suffering; God put himself on the hook, so to speak ~ on the cross, either in thought or in fact. We must go where he is and the cross is one of the places where he is. And when he sends us the sunrises, we thank him for the sunrises; when he sends us sunsets and deaths and sufferings and crosses, we thank him for that."

Lee: "I bristled. 'Is this possible, really, to thank God for the pain that befalls us?'"

Kreeft: "Yes. In heaven, we will do exactly that. We will say to God, Thank you so much for this little pain I didn't understand at the time, and that little pain that I didn't understand at the time; these I now see were the most precious things in my life."

"Even if I don't find myself emotionally capable of doing that right now, even if I cannot honestly say to God in the middle of pain, 'God, thank you for this pain,' but have to say instead, 'Deliver me from evil,' that's perfectly right and perfectly honest ~ yet I believe that's not the last word. The last words of the Lord's prayer aren't 'deliver us from evil:' the last words are, 'Thine is the glory and the honor.'"

"I think that any fairly mature Christian can look back on his or her life and identify some moment of suffering that made them much closer to God than they had ever thought possible. Before this happened, they would have said, 'I don't really see how this can accomplish any good at all,' but after they emerge from the suffering they say, 'That's amazing. I learned something I never thought I could have learned. I didn't think that my weak and rebellious will was capable of such strength, but God, with his grace, gave me the strength for a moment.' If it weren't for suffering, it wouldn't have been possible." [23]

Simply, facing and handling adversity builds character and if handled properly, will even deepen trust in God. Trust glorifies God. He is glorified when we trust Him and we let others see that trust. Paul said his difficult circumstances had turned out for greater progress of the gospel. We know there was a certain sailor who was thankful! Job said he *"learned about things too wonderful for me, which I did not know,"* Job 42:3. Did that mean he forgot all about his previous tragedies? Hardly, but he experienced deeper, more meaningful understanding than he ever dreamed!

> **Habakkuk's roots were so strong that he was not afraid to question God and wrestle with issues that tested faith**

If you would like to explore how the soul can grow through loss, then by all means read Jerry Sittser's book, A Grace Disguised.[24] Jerry and his family were driving home after a happy day trip together and due to a terrible automobile accident caused by a drunken driver, suffered the loss of his wife, his daughter and his mother all at the same time. He and three other children survived. He learned a lot about himself in the years that followed. Although we would all hope that we never have to endure such pain, we *can* go through such a tragedy and survive.

Jeremiah put it this way: *"Blessed is the man who trusts in the Lord; whose confidence is in him. He will be like a tree planted by the water that sends out its roots by the stream. It does not fear when heat comes; its leaves are always green,"* Jeremiah 17:8.

Habakkuk's roots were so strong that he was not afraid

to question God and wrestle with issues that tested faith. He was pleading with God to do something with the disobedient and sinful country of Judah. He couldn't see God working and even accused Him of not caring! God tells him that He is going to raise up Babylon to take care of Judah. He couldn't believe it! That's NOT what Habakkuk wanted to hear! Habakkuk is in a stage of grief; of disbelief. He needs to get his thinking in line with God's and God's wise, sovereign answer is:

"Because I am doing something in your days ~ You would not believe if you were told," Habakkuk 1:5.

In other words, *Habakkuk, you don't need to worry. Don't stress yourself out. I've got it all under control.* There was plenty of evil in the world around, but all of the evil in the world could not convince him there was no God. He hung onto his trust in God although he couldn't figure it out!

"It is good for me that I was afflicted, that I may learn Thy statutes," Psalm 119:71.

During a crisis, it's hard to figure things out. Thinking clearly through the shock, fear, anxiety, and numbness is a difficult task. If there's no stability to hold on to, we'll find ourselves crashing, just as in the storm. God is our standard; our stability. He is All wise; All powerful; All knowing. His Word will give us direction. We need to digest every bit of His Word possible before the crisis comes ~ and it will come ~ so we'll have something on which to draw when it happens. One of the greatest expressions of faith found anywhere is in Habakkuk 3:17-19.

"Though the fig tree should not blossom, And there be no fruit on the vines, Though the yield of the olive should fail, And the fields produce no food, Though the flock should be cut off from the fold, And there be no cattle in the stalls, Yet I will exult in the Lord, I will rejoice in the God of my salvation. The Lord God is my strength, And He has made my feet like hinds' feet, And makes me walk on my high places."

If God arrays the grass of the field and gives lilies their beautiful appearance, He will do much more for us, according to Matthew 6:33, 34. *"But seek first His kingdom and His righteousness and all these things shall be added to you."* He adds, *"therefore, do not be anxious for tomorrow; for tomorrow will care for itself. Each day has enough trouble of its own."*

Paul had anxiety relievers ~ not in the form of pills, unless he had a joy pill. He knew *"we also exult in our tribulations, knowing that tribulation brings about perseverance; and perseverance, proven character; and proven character, hope,"* Romans 5:3,4. He had the ability to look to the future and also points out that *"hope does not disappoint, because of the love of God; poured out into our hearts through the Holy Spirit."*

"So faith comes from hearing and hearing by the word of Christ," Romans 10:17.

The very fact that sin is in the world tells us the storm will hit at some point. Hopefully, adversity hasn't found you yet, but do you have a plan in place? Do you have any idea how you would handle illness if it were to strike? How you would deal with the death of a loved one? Are you learning as you help others when they have difficulty? Would you expect them to help you if the situation were reversed? Is your faith going to stabilize you during that time, or will you evacuate, not realizing that the place of safety is within your reach?

There are no hopeless situations. There are only people who have grown hopeless about them. Clare Booth Luce

As we hurried to Florida, Allen, Julie and I quoted every scripture that would come to mind. We were searching, grasping for strength. I was not only concerned for my husband who was called home from Romania, having to travel alone with this terrible anticipation, but concerned for me, being without him and not knowing what was ahead. Looking back, we can see how perfectly God orchestrated his safe return. Connections were the quickest possible for international flights. He arrived on Saturday evening. Because Jill was an organ donor, she was kept on life support until he arrived and he was able to say goodbye.

Of many favorite calming passages, one is, Isaiah 41:10 *"Fear not, for I am with you; Be not dismayed, for I am your God. I will strengthen you, Yes, I will help you, I will uphold you with My righteous right hand."*

How can a favorite Psalm even be chosen? There is so much to be gained as David speaks from his heart. *"When I am afraid, I will put my trust in Thee. In God, whose word I praise, In God I have put my trust; I shall not be afraid. What can mere man do to me?"* Psalm 56:3,4. Later, in that same Psalm, *"Thou has taken account of my wanderings; Put my tears in Thy bottle; Are they not in Thy book?"* verse 8. According to www.oldtestamentpassion.blogspot.com for Wednesday, September 5, 2007, there are several traditions regarding tear bottles. In ancient Egypt and Palestine, women had the habit of collecting the tears shed during mourning, and storing them in bottles. Sometimes the bottles were buried with the deceased, and another legend is that when the tears in the bottle dried up, the mourning period was over. What touching thought the Psalmist brings about in this beautiful word picture, depicting God as being so aware of our suffering that He collects our tears in a flask or bottle.

You, too, can practice comforting when you see the opportunity and it will not only strengthen you, but give strength and hope to those to whom you are ministering. Help your grieving friends by sharing your favorite faith building passages, explaining how the trials will get better and outlooks will be more positive in time. Don't preach. Just share. God hears us and is ready to help, even if it is not all grasped at first. God gives comfort. We receive it. We give comfort. Someone else receives it. Comfort is available should we again be in need. Praise God for His complete planning for our well being.

Questions for study and discussion:

1. Compare preparations for physical and spiritual storms.

2. Make a list of your most meaningful faith building scriptures.

3. When going about your daily routine, bring back to memory as many details as you can of the *heroes of faith*.

4. Discuss proper medications for anxiety.

5. Discuss the source of the strength of favorite Bible heroes.

For further study:
The Power of Suffering by John MacArthur, Jr.[25]

11

Slow Me Down so I can Pray

"After He had sent the crowds away, He went upon the mountain by Himself to pray; and when it was evening, He was there alone," Matthew 14:23.

Being on the grieving fast track, I was trying to fill my time by staying busy, when the thought from a daily spiritual calendar jumped out at me:

> *Lord, I often run here and there seeking help and comfort. Please give me the courage to stop running and come to you in prayer.*

It's not surprising that we run out of steam during times of crisis. Being out of our spiritual routine for any reason can create a void in our lives. During the heat of the moment, the phrase *Lord, please help me,* may be the best approach, as the frazzled mind just won't let the words come. Others may actually do their best at expressing agonies to God during these fragile, confusing times. I remember looking out the window of the hospital waiting room, very early in the morning, being confused as to what I could pray for at the time. We weren't given any hope, yet we do have a God of all power. On the other hand, if her life could not be normal, was life really best? Back to my dad's philosophy: *God will do the very best thing.* And He did. Prayer tends to be more frequent and more meaningful when backed into a corner and we're feeling powerless in our circumstances. Although we're usually much too impatient, the most appropriate prayer may be, *Lord, Your will be done* ~ and then wait.

The best prayers often have more groans than words. John Bunyon

When confronted with seemingly insurmountable situations, Nehemiah's prayers revealed a lot about his elationship with God. Jerusalem was still in his heart, even though his body was in captivity in Babylon. When bad news had been brought to him about the peril of the Jews in Jerusalem, Nehemiah sat down, mourned and wept, fasting and praying. Take time to read his prayer in the first chapter of the book, noticing how he addresses God. He knew the value of lengthy petitions (verses 5-11), as well as a short, hurried request ~ almost a breath between the two verses, Nehemiah 2:4, 5. He knew that praying and waiting go hand in hand and prayers in this book reveal a lot about how Nehemiah gained his exceptional leadership qualities. The faith and determination with which he prayed kept him grounded and directed even amidst adversity, ridicule, bullying and threats. Adversity tends to be more *refining* than a life of ease, and Nehemiah was being refined. He appreciated the value of prayer.

We hesitate. We doubt. We spend too much time trying to figure out details, wondering why some prayers are answered and others are not. (The *why* question again!) There are no magic answers to our wonderings. We may have prayed with great faith, putting all our energies into communication with God; we may have struggled with the right words, being unable to express our longings but confident that the Holy Spirit will intercede and interpret our message.

"And in the same way the Spirit also helps our weakness; for we do not know how to pray as we should, but the Spirit Himself intercedes for us with groanings too deep for words...," Romans 8:26.

And then there's the wait. Waiting for a decision is miserable. (Remember the suspense when our children were little and they were waiting to receive some surprise we had promised?) We know or at least we think we know what we need ~ why doesn't God grant it? We want a vending machine answer. We did put in our prayer, didn't we? Now, may I have the answer? I wonder how Abraham stood it, waiting 25 years for a promise to be kept! He certainly didn't feel *betrayed* by God. What a clever tool of Satan to dupe us into believing God doesn't care.

Notice what Edwin Crozier has to say about our requests made to God, in his book, <u>Plugged In: High Voltage Prayer</u>.

"Supplication is not our genie in the lamp. We do not get our every desire just by rubbing the magic prayer lamp. Matthew 6:10 says, 'Your will be done on earth as it is in heaven.' Even our supplication should not be done to accomplish our will, but God's. This governs everything else we learn about prayer. Our overriding concern must be that God is glorified and His will be done. When Moses interceded for Israel in Exodus 32:11-14, the prayer was about God's glory, not Israel's salvation. In Psalm 74, Asaph prayed for Judah's deliverance but the reason was that God would be glorified. Supplication is not spiritual manipulation. God explained in Isaiah 43:13 that He works and we cannot reverse it. We cannot pressure God to do our will. We may simply ask Him to take our prayer into account." [26]

Faith brings us to petition God for our wants and needs, but would we be in a healthy spiritual place if all our prayers were answered? Suppose they *were* all answered, would we still feel the need to pray? Or would the headiness of the answers lead us to feel some false power instead of giving God the glory? Would we end up using prayer for our own interests, asking for bigger and better things instead of wanting to align our will to God's? Do we pray selfishly? Do we wait for a crisis to pray at all?

When we're helping a grieving friend and answers are just not available, it helps to be able to ask God for assistance ~ for patience, wisdom and strength to bear whatever is before us. Faithful hearts that are pouring out to God find cleansing relief.

Too often we want to be in *cheer up* mode, and try to turn their thoughts to other subjects, just so we won't have to address any difficult questions. We don't want them to say anything negative or express any doubts. *Shhhh. You need to be strong!* Do we really think God doesn't know our troubled thoughts? How can God be *"a rock of habitation to which I may ntinually come"* (Psalm 71:3) if we're afraid to approach Him with our doubts and struggles? Perhaps a tongue that has not praised God feels uncomfortable bringing burdens to Him? Or we may be thinking that God will not hear our prayers because of some sin in our lives. Be aware that there's little rationale in the mind of the grief stricken. Thoughts may or may not be coherent.

"When I pondered to understand this, It was troublesome in my sight until I came into the sanctuary of God...," Psalm 73:16,17a.

> **Perhaps a tongue that has not praised God feels un-comfortable bringing burdens to Him?**

Some of the most moving passages of Scripture reveal our heroes of faith, pouring their hearts out to God. David, in Psalm 51, asked to be cleansed from sin; admitted his sin and wanted to regain joy and gladness. *"Restore to me the joy of Thy salvation."* Then he wanted to teach others. Those heroes emptied their hearts before Him and they too, were afraid He wasn't listening, Habakkuk 1:2.

Isaiah had some stern things to say to the nation of Israel about their habit of fasting just to be noticed, Isaiah 58. They mistreated their neighbors and then wondered why God wasn't listening. Isaiah 59: 2 says, *"But your iniquities have made a separation between you and your God, And your sins have hidden His face from you, so that He does not hear."*

Through our actions, are our prayers hindered? They can be. Husbands are admonished to live with their wives in an understanding way...so that their prayers will not be hindered, 1 Peter 3:7. The way we live our lives certainly has bearing on our spirituality. We may feel close to God and we may not. We have to be careful, though, about adopting the idea that God will answer all our prayers if our lives are focused on Him and we say all the right words with the right motives. Job apparently used that formula and was not spared difficulty. Before His betrayal, when Jesus prayed to *let this cup pass* (Matthew 26:39), would we dare say His prayer was not motivated correctly? The cup didn't pass. We sometimes forget the last part of that verse, *"not as I will, but as Thou wilt."* His Father's plan didn't eliminate His suffering.

> **Are we patient enough, strong enough to let God work in His own time?**

God is simply on a different level and works according to His own plan, using life's tragedies to bring His word into focus in our lives. Again, I didn't say He *causes* life's tragedies. God is Sovereign, loving and merciful and our faith that He will bring about the best in a situation helps us to be able to cope and persevere. His purposes WILL be accomplished. Paul accepted the Lord's answer to his unanswered prayers about his *thorn in the flesh* and found ways to rejoice, 2 Corinthians 12:9-10. And what did God say? *"My grace is sufficient for you ~ for power is perfected in weakness."* He learned to *"be anxious for nothing, but in everything by prayer and supplication with thanksgiving let your requests be made known to God,"* Philippians 4:4-6. That in itself brings *"peace that will guard our hearts and minds in Christ* Jesus," Philippians 4:7.

There's relief to be found when we can lay our problems at the feet of Jesus. When we know we have prayed according to God's plan, there's rest!

Looking at Habakkuk again, after God outlines the plan He has for Judah, Habakkuk 2:1-2 says, *"I will stand on my guard post and station myself on the rampart; And I will keep watch to see what He will speak to me, And how I may reply when I am reproved."* I wonder what his countenance was as he was speaking. Did he have his hands on his hips or his arms folded with a *we'll see* attitude or was it more a curiosity wondering *how is God going to work this out?* I know we can't know that but as he prays for God's mercy in chapter three, we see the deep trusting faith of Habakkuk. Sure, he's afraid *"I hear and my body trembles"* (3:16 RSV), but he doesn't let that fear take root and concludes with *"I will rejoice in the God f my salvation. The Lord God is my strength,"* 3:18-19.

Are we patient enough, strong enough to let God work n His own time? Can we bring ourselves to thank God for he good that suffering can bring? Maybe not right away, but eventually blessings can be seen, even in tragedy. Jill never had to know she was ill, and we have learned to count that as a blessing. God can be praised when those who die suddenly do not have to suffer. Anyone who has had to nurse a loved one through a long and painful, lingering illness knows what a blessing it would be to pass quickly. There are lessons to be learned through physical pain and we cannot know why some linger in death and why some do not but we can, at the end, do as Habakkuk and rejoice that the Lord God is our strength.

The blessings that God delivers to us after tragedy, help to make it more bearable. If we're not bitter, we realize that good does come out of chaos. We are the determining factor ~ the receptacle ~ the pot being formed on the potter's wheel that shapes our usefulness. How sad, should we go through life's difficulties and fail to learn from them!

"But now, O Lord, Thou art our Father, We are the clay, and Thou our potter; And all of us are the work of Thy hand," Isaiah 64:8.

Our family is not the same and never will be. Our hearts are torn with any report of a parent who loses a child. Sad reports of soldiers lost during the war in Iraq mean there are grief stricken families somewhere. Even now, these many years later, we still have an occasional bad day, but there have been opportunities to speak, to teach, and to help others that may or may not have come about otherwise. Frank just completed his 12th teaching trip to Romania. (There were some nervous days the first time he decided to return. I couldn't help but wonder if something else would happen.) When a friend loses a sister or brother, our three sons have developed a compassion and understanding that even helps them in their chosen professions. God is the author of comfort for His people. *"As one whom his mother comforts, so I will comfort you,"* Isaiah 66:13.

Maybe Habakkuk did have his hands on his hips; but with a smile and a knowing nod, a confidence that faithful prayer can bring, everything *would* work out.

> *"When I pondered to understand this, it was troublesome in my sight until I came into the sanctuary of God..."* Psalm 73:16,17a.

> *"The Lord is in His holy temple. Let all the earth be silent before Him,"* Habakkuk 2:20.

If Jesus needed that connection to God how much more do we?

Habakkuk had a relationship of trust with his God. If we have a relationship of trust with others, we absolutely refuse to believe something bad about them until we have sufficient reason to do otherwise. Philip Yancey, in Reaching for the Invisible God, has this to say regarding trust:

> *Over time, both through personal experiences and my study of the Bible, I have come to know certain qualities of God as well. God's style often baffles me: he moves at a slow pace, prefers rebels and prodigals, restrains his power, and speaks in whispers and silence. Yet even in these qualities I see evidence of his longsuffering, mercy, and desire to woo rather than compel. When in doubt, I focus on Jesus, the most unfiltered revelation of God's own self. I have learned to trust God, and when some tragedy or evil occurs that I cannot synthesize with the God I have come to know and love, then I look to other explanations.* [27]

Trust can be gained through more study, especially on prayer. Are you happy with your prayer life? Many of us are not. Just before Jesus chose the Apostles, He went to the mountain to pray and spent the whole night in prayer to God, Luke 6:12. If Jesus needed that connection to God how much more do we? Hopefully, we do realize our need to know and understand more about prayer ~ to be more closely connected ~ to understand His will and to align ourselves accordingly. If we're connected to God through prayer, life's burdens will be lighter.

"*But to this one I will look, To him who is humble and contrite of spirit, and who trembles at My word,*" Isaiah 66:2.

Paul, in all of his positive wisdom, puts it all in perspective in Romans 8:18. "*For I consider that the sufferings of this present time are not worthy to be compared with the glory that is to be revealed to us.*"

When a person is at his wits end, it is not a cowardly thing to pray. It is the only way to get into touch with Reality.
Oswald Chambers

Questions for study and discussion:

1. Describe the relationship between Nehemiah and God.

2. What should be our attitude when we petition God?

3. How should we deal with our doubts?

4. What can hinder active prayer life?

5. Discuss lessons learned from God's answer to Paul and our failure to get the answers we expected.

12

Contentment and Joy

"A joyful heart makes a cheerful face, but when the heart is sad, the spirit is broken," Proverbs 15:13.

Remember how accomplished we can feel after completing a project? That peaceful, all is right with the world feeling makes us so content! Mental pictures of contentment may be the calm that comes on a fall day after a long, hot summer, or curling up in a window seat with a cup of hot tea and a stack of books. It may be giving our homes a good spring cleaning or getting some of that yard work accomplished. Sitting on the swing outdoors on a perfect spring day, just relaxing and listening to the sounds of nature will do it for others.

When Paul wrote to Timothy, he explained that *"godliness actually is a means of great gain, when accompanied with contentment. For we have brought nothing into the world, so we cannot take anything out of it either. And if we have food and covering, with these we shall be content,"* 1 Timothy 6:6-8.

In a cemetery in England stands a grave marker with this inscription: SHE DIED FOR WANT OF THINGS. Alongside that sign is another which reads: HE DIED TRYING TO GIVE THEM TO HER. Our lack of patience and the constant desire for things doesn't necessarily shout contentment!

Spiritually, we may think we have a good handle on our prayer life; have daily Bible reading under our belts; try to attend to the needs of others as well as to our family and even teach a few classes ~ being generally satisfied with our efforts, but all the while, knowing there is room for improvement. And then there's the flip side. All was going well until the world of grief or illness is either directly or indirectly on your doorstep and dealing with it is one of the most difficult experiences of our life. The flip side; anxiety, lack of patience, confusion, fear and grief becomes all too real. It's safe to say that if contentment has not been developed in everyday life, then contentment will not be found in times of grief. Where is peace and how do we get back to that comfort zone?

As mentioned in chapter four, being comforted is usually something that is external; something that is done to you or for you by someone else. You may be physically comforted by a big bowl of creamy grits and butter ~ or a big piece of chocolate cake (now that we've found out chocolate is actually good for us!). Contentment comes from within. Godly contentment is being controlled by what is <u>within you</u> in times of stress, instead of by your circumstances.

> **Paul had an ability to focus on the Gospel instead of his personal pain and suffering**

After suffering tragedy, some adopt the stoical approach, training themselves to never react, either to good or bad in order to avoid more hurt, and that just seems like such a tragic way to live. Isn't life to be enjoyed? Grievers sometimes fall into the *I'll never be happy again*, type of negative thinking. Surely, we should do more than merely *survive* life's trials. Life goes by too quickly to be stuck in grief. What a waste if our usefulness to others as well as to God is diminished. Looking for ways to be useful and recognizing blessings will make every day count, instead of just counting the days.

Solomon certainly tasted the drudgery of living when he wrote, *"So I hated life for the work which had been done under the sun was grievous to me; because everything is futility and striving after the wind,"* Ecclesiastes 2:17. Later, he also wrote, *"In the day of prosperity be happy, but in the day of adversity consider ~ God has made the one as well as the other...,"* Ecclesiastes 7:14.

Paul said he had learned to be content in his circumstances. He developed it; it didn't come naturally. If we haven't learned the art of contentment, we can wear ourselves out mentally, physically and spiritually. Paul had an ability to focus on the Gospel instead of his personal pain and suffering. Self-pity was unknown to him. How many of us would be praying and singing after being beaten and thrown into prison?

Consider Elijah for a moment, my very favorite Bible character. Remember the account of Elijah and the prophets of Baal; the contest on Mt. Carmel? Elijah was at the top. He had mightily called down God's power; the sacrifice, the altar, the water in the trenches were all consumed with fire, but after it was over, Ahab's wicked queen Jezebel, vowed to take Elijah's life and he ran scared ~ terrified, alone, depressed and weakened. The mighty display of faith that just happened now crumbles. He's falling apart and wants to die, thinking he's the only one left that serves God. What a drastic change of events! But look at what happens. God attends to Elijah, letting him rest and then sends an angel to feed him. For forty days afterward, Elijah was escaping, en route to Mt. Horeb ~ the area we know as Sinai. It's in Judah! A good distance south of Mt. Carmel. Listen to what Bob & Sandra Waldron point out in their commentary on the Divided Kingdom and the Prophets of that period, <u>Till there was no remedy</u>, 1 Kings 19.

> *"Do you notice that forty days passed from the time Elijah left the point a day's journey south of Beersheba until God spoke to him at Mt. Horeb? That means God was allowing time itself to act as a healer for Elijah's discouragement. There was reason to grieve for the nation of Israel, and God allowed time for Elijah to grieve. But grieving alone would not solve Israel's problems. It was not as hopeless as Elijah thought it was. Notice God's next actions. He spoke to Elijah, asking him why he was there instead of back home in Israel. But, do you notice, He did not rebuke Elijah for his discouragement? Instead He demonstrated His might over nature. (That was the account where He told Elijah to stand on the mountain and the wind, an earthquake and a fire passed by.) He was reminding Elijah that God was in control. He would care for His prophet."* [28]

We need those reminders. Recovery doesn't happen all at once. Perhaps we'd be wise to use the 40 days as a guide and tell ourselves and those we're trying to help, that in 40 days, our outlook will be somewhat different. There is a place for grief ~ it serves a useful purpose. Grieving and being able to express it is important to recovery. Grief that is stuffed inside only appears in more complicated ways at a later time. It's just important that it doesn't take control. God instilled a wonderful comfort system in our brothers and sisters and we should not only give that comfort, but in our own times of distress, should drop our pride and take full advantage of it.

> It's been my experience that we as Christians have little patience with someone who has trouble getting back into the game

God's prescription of rest, food and time should be remembered. Jesus knew the value of taking time to repair, often going to quiet places to be by himself. Please remember too, friends, that your timetable for recovery may be totally different from someone else's. It's been my experience that we as Christians have little patience with someone who has trouble getting back into the game. Forty days may give a different perspective, but it will not end grief. We tend to expect them to be *over it* in a few months, and it just doesn't happen. Even if everything seems to be good on the outside, be assured that there are lots of bad days and times that grief will wash over the griever like fresh dew. These responses are typical, especially during the first year.

There are certain processes that can bring order back to our lives and it's not as easy as picking up a few toys or putting away the laundry. There are physical things to be dealt with; personal belongings; legal things ~ and some find that very painful, but having to deal with those things can be very beneficial. It helps to bring us back to a place of normalcy.

If you have scrapbooking talents, offer to help preserve

family photos. This can be very therapeutic, giving an opportunity for the griever to reminisce. There may be tears, but don't panic. Tears are cleansing. Listen to their stories. If some of the photos are showing signs of deterioration, take them to be copied; it can add years to the life of a photo and you will have helped to create a treasure.

Being involved in a project will help to occupy the mind if re-establishing order seems to be a problem; something that will not only distract but uplift. This is the time to focus on healing. Since most of us are generally overly committed, set aside other responsibilities if need be. Some of us just don't know how to say no but this is a time to draw near to God; to His Word, and to associations with good people. Seek it and do it. Request it! If for some reason, one attempt doesn't work out, try again soon.

Remember the work in the resource room? It was good to have that focus. Trying to do volunteer work left me too frayed as patience had grown really thin. Just have to have those ducks in step, you know, so it was just best that I worked alone for a while. If there had been another child at home to care for, there would have been another need; a different focus. Some peace was found in the *orderliness* of working on the project, but when that last year was completed, the grief, even though I tried to keep it hidden, became even more prominent. Things kept happening. Our house had been robbed and vandalized, requiring extensive repair. There were deaths in our church family. An uncle died. The cat broke its leg. (Silly, isn't it? I held up fairly well during Jill's funeral and was having a meltdown because her cat broke its leg!) Murphy's law had caught up with us; a day without a crisis was a total loss. To complicate things, when my brother's wife died very suddenly in March of 1995, I flew to Alabama to attend the funeral, but found myself extremely weakened by this event.

My husband's mother, incapacitated with a stroke for some time, died two weeks later. I felt great sadness, for her youngest daughter had died too, at an early age, and when I could have benefited from her experience, she wasn't able to communicate. Just a few days after her death, on April 19 he bombing in Oklahoma City took place and I cried for days. Depression had found its place. I was fatigued, weakened and couldn't be trusted with important information because I couldn't remember it! Being convinced I'd be stuck in this unhappiness forever, I was existing through life instead of living it and I hated it. As David in Psalm 6, I was weary with sighing and tears.

God's providence steps in. If it had not been for our oldest son's upcoming wedding in May of that year, I may have continued in that unhappy place, but there was happiness on the horizon! Even though the pain was not erased, being with family and rejoicing in Randy's and Jerrell's new life together brought me to a different place with at least the possibility of contentment. Be sure to take note of the life situations of a griever and the circumstances surrounding the death of his or her loved one, as many things contribute to anxiety and may hinder progress. Any additional difficulty, however small, may exacerbate grief.

Being content does not mean feeling no emotional pain. Even through tears and distress, trials can be faced with the contentment of knowing God is in control, and He has not forgotten us in our time of trial.

Gary Henry points out in <u>Brass Tacks</u> on Psalm 4, *that as God's people, our expectations are sometimes too low. When we face problems, about the most we expect to receive from God is courage, but with God's help we can have not only courage but joy and gladness.*

David's confidence in what he would receive, in Psalm 4, is impressive. *"Answer me when I call, O God of my righteousness! Thou hast relieved me in my distress; Be gracious to me and hear my prayer."* After a comment to his enemies, he reveals the source of that confidence. *"But know that the Lord has set apart the godly man for Himself, The Lord hears when I call to Him. Tremble and do not sin; Meditate in your heart upon your bed, and* be still. Offer the sacrifices of righteousness, and trust in the Lord." When others ask who will show them any good, David asks the Lord to shine His countenance upon them and continues, "*Thou hast put gladness in my heart...in peace I will both lie down and sleep, For Thou alone, O Lord, dost make me to dwell in safety.*" [29]

The Psalms are so unique in their instruction. David knows the tendency to mull over worrisome thoughts after getting in bed and his notation is to meditate. God has put gladness in his heart and he sleeps in peace. Peaceful sleep. Ironic, isn't it, that America spends millions yearly on sleep meds and David has the solution.

> **Ironic, isn't it, that America spends millions yearly on sleep meds and David has the solution**

David obviously spent a lot of time with God. With a little practice, studying the Psalms will become more meaningful to us as well. Scripture and prayer will sustain us through many difficulties; there *are* promises that extend beyond the pain. Many of the Psalms reveal the pain of the writer. (If not for times of grief, there surely wouldn't be as many poets!) While you're reading through the Psalms, begin to observe how many of them were born through that pain. David was deeply spiritual and didn't get mad at God when his child was dying. He prayed and fasted persistently until God gave the answer. When that answer came, he accepted it. He got up, attended to personal hygiene and worshiped God, even before he returned to his own house to eat. Failing to praise God was out of the question. He had the ability to let go of the past ~ not the memories, but the sadness. His joy was returning, 2 Samuel 12:13-23. It's notable that his servants did not understand his grief. Be sure to read the entire account and note their confusion. How would we deal with a similar situation?

"*Weeping may endure for a night, but joy comes in the morning,*" Psalm 30:5.

Sometimes we fail to be content because we lack the patience to let God do the work in His way. There's control again, this time manifesting itself in a bad way. We don't actually think God will come through for us. That patience would bring contentment ~ if only we would let it.

In John 16:19-22, Jesus was talking to his disciples, telling them that in a little while, He would leave and they would have sorrow. They didn't understand what He meant! He told them their sorrow would turn to joy and even used the example of a woman in childbirth. Any woman knows that when that baby comes, the sorrow is overcome with the joy but the part that struck me was verse 22. *"Therefore you too now have sorrow; but I will see you again, and your heart will rejoice, and <u>no one takes your joy away from you</u>..."* What joy there will be when we finally give up this troublesome earth to see the One who promises us complete and unlimited joy.

After a major life trauma, joy is not something that will just automatically appear but as time goes on, and a measure of contentment has returned, focus can be given to others. If a griever still seems to be too inwardly focused, suggestion can be made to think of one thing each day that can be done for someone else. In the beginning, it may be as simple as a positive thought, a phone call or a card. Verbal good wishes take a little more effort, as well as being difficult emotionally, but if positive thoughts are shared, those thoughts will take root and grow. Outward thoughts versus inward thoughts help to break the cycle of grieving.

Find ways to instill laughter. The antics of children can bring some chuckles. Watch reruns of <u>I Love Lucy</u> or <u>Mayberry RFD</u>. Do things that will make God happy; it'll make you happy too. Administering to others brings happiness and satisfaction. Forgive or ask forgiveness if it is needed. When we give what we have to give, then we will receive what we need.

"Give, and it will be given to you; good measure, pressed down, shaken together, running over, they will pour into your lap," Luke 6:38.

Be grateful we live in a free country where daily needs are plentiful. Gratitude and thanksgiving are like healing ointments. It's hard to be sad or angry and thankful at the same time!

Notice Paul's instruction in 1 Thessalonians 5.

Verse 14: ...*encourage* the fainthearted, help the weak, be patient with all men.
Verse 16: *Rejoice* always.

Verse 17: *Pray* without ceasing.

Verse 18: In everything *give thanks* ~ for this is God's will for you.

Surely Paul is not saying grievers can be thankful for these traumatic events! Why not? Paul was thankful! Who knows the future? My aunt's sister, prone to strokes, was murdered. As horrible as it was, her sudden death may have been much more merciful than a long lingering life of disability.

"A man has joy in an apt answer and how delightful is a timely word!" Proverbs 15:23.

A fable

There was an old Chinese farmer who had one horse and one son. One day the horse jumped out of the corral and fled to the hills. When he could not be found the neighbors came and exclaimed, *Your horse got out. What bad luck!* The old Chinaman quickly replied, *How do you know it is bad luck?*

Interestingly, the next day, the horse returned to his usual place of watering and feeding ~ leading twelve wild stallions with him. When the farmer's son saw them in the corral, he slipped out and locked the gate. A few days later the son was trying to break one of the wild stallions when he was thrown off, breaking one of his legs. The neighbors came again and sorrowfully expressed, *Your son broke his leg. What bad luck!* In a familiar reply his father said, *How do you know it is bad luck?*

True to form, a short time later a Chinese warlord came through the town and conscripted every able bodied young man, taking them off to war ~ never to return. However, due to the broken leg, the farmer's son was not compelled to go.[30]

These things can steal joy and happiness

1) Lingering in the memories.
2) Not getting proper rest and restorative sleep.
3) Poor health habits; failure to eat properly.
4) Failure to count blessings.
5) Bitterness toward God.
6) Sin that separates you from God.

The measure of success is not whether you have a tough problem to deal with, but whether it's the same problem you had last year. John Foster Dulles

Even many years later, there are things that can bring joy as well as a fresh tear. While at the annual Florida College lectureship in 2006, I saw a friend of Jill's that I hadn't seen in quite a while. As we talked, he pulled out his billfold and said, *I want to show you something.* He flipped to a high school picture of Jill and said, *I keep this with me all the time, just to remind me of the brevity of life.* I was deeply and genuinely touched. It gave me such joy to know that her friends remember and use her memory as a challenge for themselves. Others share their memories, too ~ we do not grieve alone. Don't be sad if in sharing or helping a griever, a tear appears. Remember, tears are cleansing. Maybe enough tears can make rainbows! Even if a tear comes, kind memories can instill joy and hope!

Contentment and joy may be just around the corner and they may appear in unique ways. God blesses us in so many ways, and life is to be enjoyed.

"Trust in the Lord with all our hearts and lean not on our own understanding; in all our ways acknowledge Him and He shall direct our paths," Proverbs 3:5-6.

Life is SO worth living.

Questions for study and discussion:

1. Discuss the difference between contentment and comfort.

2. What is the stoical approach toward grief?

3. How did God deal with Elijah's discouragement?

4. Discuss some lessons we can learn about grief from the Psalms.

5. Discuss things that can deprive us of happiness.

6. Compare the confusion of David's servants as he was grieving to our confusion in helping the grieving.

What a Friend We Have in Jesus **13**
All our Sins & Griefs to Bear

"Surely our griefs He Himself bore, and our sorrows He carried," Isaiah 53:4a.

The ability to withstand the trials and problems of life is certainly made easier by friends; friends who would gladly take some of your pain, if they only could. We probably all have a mental picture of someone who is our true friend, and sadly, we probably also have remembrances of some friendships that didn't work out so well. Aristotle said *a friend is a single soul dwelling in two bodies.* Walter Winchell said *a real friend is the one who walks in when the rest of the world walks out.* I like that.

According to <u>101 Hymn Stories</u>,[31] by Kenneth W. Osbeck, Joseph Scriven wrote the song, <u>*What a friend we have in Jesus*</u>, in 1857. He was born in Dublin, Ireland, but at age 25 left his native country and migrated to Canada. One of the reasons for his leaving was the accidental drowning of his fiancée on the day before their wedding. He probably needed a change of scenery as he struggled with his grief.

When he wrote these words, they were never intended for publication; he wrote them when he learned of his mother's serious illness. It was too far to go home for a visit, so he included these words in a letter of comfort to her. Some time later, when he was ill, a friend saw the words on a tablet laying next to his bedside. The friend asked Scriven if he had written the words and he replied: T*he Lord and I did it between us.*

Joseph had endeared himself to the people of the area, often cutting wood for widows who had no means for payment. His skills were noticed by others who wanted to hire him, but they were told *you can't hire that man. He only works for those who cannot pay.*

After his death, the citizens of Port Hope, Ontario erected a monument in his memory, and on his gravestone are the words to this song. Just knowing this background may help us understand the depth of his words.

God's plan for Jesus to be our friend and Savior started at the beginning of time. Prophecies of Jesus begin in Genesis 3 and continue for centuries. Jesus is coming; and with His coming, He will bear our sins and our griefs.

A study of the life of Christ reveals that when He entered this world, He suffered all the things that we may suffer, not because He didn't already understand but so we could be convinced that He *does* understand. He understands, not only trials but joys as well. We are free to take our joys, our trials, our requests to our Lord in prayer.

Oh, what peace we often forfeit. O what needless pain we bear, all because we do not carry, everything to God in prayer.

We can lay anything at the feet of Jesus. Jesus knows our differences and our various needs. He knows our frame, Psalm 103:14. Just look at His choosing of the apostles. They were all different! They didn't have perfect understanding; some were skeptical, some were pessimistic, and even reluctant to serve Him. You can see His wisdom in doing this; the apostles were just plain, ordinary men but their important quality was an honest heart that was open to truth.

John MacArthur discusses this in his very perceptive book, Twelve Ordinary Men.[32] He notes how each apostle died. Only the death of James is mentioned in Scripture; in Acts 12, when he was killed by Herod, but history and tradition tell us that all the others were martyred as well, except for John; the writer of the gospel of John, 1,2,3rd John and Revelation. He was the only apostle who lived to old age.

Do you think he ever wondered about that? Did he wonder why he lived and why the others didn't? Do you think he ever questioned his purpose in life?

Many of us do question, especially as we grow older, but God knows that a dedicated, aged faithful Christian is one of the most beautiful and outstanding examples. John was left alone on the isle of Patmos, in a prison atmosphere. There was personal loss involved for Him. It was his brother, James, who was killed by Herod; killed for his faith. He had lost a brother as well as other close friends and he was left alone. For some of us that would be the most painful existence of all.

Jesus loved this friend, this apostle, and years before when they were together He consistently taught him about love through His own life and example, until John is known as the apostle of love. John was one of the *sons of thunder*. Now you can use whatever mental image that comes to mind on that, but surely he didn't get that reputation because of his love! This alone should convince us that we're not failures in the eyes of Jesus just because we have made mistakes. Jesus had a plan for John and whatever grief came his way because he was the last surviving apostle, Jesus helped him bear. No one was ever reluctant to approach Jesus for fear of being rejected. John somehow knew that just one glimpse of Jesus in the fullness of His glory will be worth all the pain and sorrow and suffering that he endured.

Do we realize that in our own lives? What do we do when we're isolated or in a difficult situation? Maybe life has handed you lemons and you don't have that lemonade recipe yet. Sadness and unhappiness in our lives may be for various reasons. Maybe you've suffered severe financial failure or business losses. It could be that you are unmarried and alone and there is no one special on the horizon. It could be that you want to start a family and it just isn't happening. Or maybe you *do* have a family and it has been changed forever by illness or death. How about the winter years? Are you there yet? Perhaps the physical pain and aching is just not as you expected or maybe sin has gotten a grip on your life and the list could go on and on with things relative to pain and death, illness and jealousy and envy; so many difficult things in this life.

Some are no fault of our own and some have been

brought on by our own sin, and as a result we may question or blame God. It reminds me of the young woman who was sleeping around and when she became pregnant, she said, *God, why did you let this happen?!* Placing blame is easier than repenting! Regardless of the sin, we can be forgiven but the consequence of that sin may remain.

> *Can we find a friend so faithful who will all our sorrows share?*

Do we realize what a friend Jesus is, even in those times? Think back to Stephen in Acts 7. We read how Stephen was teaching and preaching in Jerusalem and then arrested for doing so. He stood before the Sanhedrin and gave a mini history lesson to those jealous Jewish leaders. Even though they were convicted by his words, they didn't like what they were hearing. Their anger was just out of control. He was thrown out of the city and stoned to death.

We could again ask *why*, but have a glimpse of how Jesus cares for us. Scripture says Stephen was gazing intently into heaven and he saw the glory of God and Jesus *standing* at the right hand of God. This is the only place in Scripture to my knowledge that Jesus is standing; all others mention Him *sitting* at the right hand of God. That just gives me the idea that Jesus is up on His feet, witnessing what is being done to His servant and being eager to protect; wanting to give comfort and support. Do you remember that because of this one event the church was scattered abroad, and that persecution is what took the gospel to many distant areas? No, I don't think God caused Stephen's death just so the gospel could spread, but He uses the events of this life for His purpose.

Consider this story found in a recent church bulletin:

> As a Christian was traveling by train to his homeland of Hungary, a communist customs agent came through checking baggage. A sack of Bibles sat at our brother's feet. By his side lay his own personal Bible with notes and sermon outlines. The customs agent looked at the sack first, opened

it and began to throw the Bibles out of the window of the speeding train. As if for spite, the agent looked down at the open, used and obviously personal Bible of our brother, grabbed it and also threw it out the window. For three years our brother bemoaned the fact that his good Bible with so many notes and sermons was missing; no longer his constant companion. He believed Romans 8:28, but couldn't understand how this could work out for good.

One day he received his Bible through the mail with the enclosed letter.

That's what Jesus does. He provides; heals the broken hearted and binds up their wounds

Dear brother in Christ: Thank you, thank you for the use of your Bible. I found it by the railroad three years ago. I have kept it, read it, and studied it often. My family and I have written many Scriptures down on paper and many more in our hearts. We cannot thank you enough for now maybe we can go to heaven...But brother, please forgive me for keeping your Bible so long. I thought that if I did not read it now, I might never again find a Bible to read.[33]

"And we know that God causes all things to work together for good to those who love God, to those who are called according to His purpose," Romans 8:28.

Psalm 147 begins with praise to the Lord and verse 3 says *"He heals the broken hearted and binds up their wounds."* Psalm 145 says *"The Lord is gracious and full of compassion, slow to anger and great in mercy. The Lord is good to all, and His tender mercies are over all His works,"* vs. 8-9, NKJV.

That's what Jesus does. He provides; heals the broken hearted and binds up their wounds. His Word brings comfort, just as with Habakkuk. Just knowing that Habakkuk questioned

God made me feel better. The Word can bring peace if we spend enough time with it.

> **Suppose you've prayed and prayed about your situation and you're still stuck with whatever it is**

In His arms he'll take and shield thee, thou wilt find a solace there.

Suppose you've prayed and prayed about your situation and you're still stuck with whatever it is. We can look at that two ways: we can selfishly ask the Lord to *take the suffering away* or we can ask Him to give us strength to endure it. There's a cross stitch in my bathroom, where it'll be noticed daily, that says, *We're not promised an easy life ~ we're promised help to live it.*

Christians, women especially, are like a box of toothpicks. Take each toothpick alone and try to break it, and it will easily break in two. Glue all those toothpicks together, and it's impossible to break them. The glue has become solid and strengthened that mass of toothpicks. The glue could represent friends, who bind with us in order to survive life's trials, but I like to think of the glue as God's Word. It is the basis of what bonds us together and keeps us from breaking. If we don't know it, how can we be strengthened by it?

> **You know, you can't shut your garage door and not answer the phone and then criticize friends for not helping when you are depressed**

The important thing for us is to not only know it but to put it into practice. Do you make a good comforter or do you stay away in fear of saying or doing the wrong thing? Don't stay away and leave a toothpick all alone! You don't have to say a word. Just be there.

But what if you were not comforted in your grief? Maybe no one helped you or maybe you just weren't cooperative. You know, you can't shut your garage door and not answer the phone and then criticize friends for not helping when you are depressed.

Even when you don't have answers, can you still serve Him? Would it be enough to just receive God's grace? Remember, grace is receiving things we don't deserve and remember too, that God told Paul *my grace is sufficient for thee.*

When we were at the 2006 lectureship at Florida College, the singing for the last night was centered around the resurrection. The planning of it was powerful and the singing of it was magnificent. Each thought led to another and as I sat there, I thought, wouldn't it be enough that Christ died on the cross for our sins? Even if we have to live until eternity without knowing the answers to questions that plague us, isn't the sacrifice of Jesus enough? How can we say it wouldn't be! The Lamb of God was sacrificed ~ for all of us ~ once for all time. Jesus is our mediator and we have the incredible privilege of being able to approach God on His throne through prayer.

> Jesus learned obedience from the things He suffered so it would be sad if we didn't learn from our trials

Several years ago, Randy's and Jerrell's house burned. It was a total loss and had to be gutted and rebuilt. Building delays and red tape kept them in an apartment for a year where surroundings were unfamiliar and safety for their boys was a concern. We can only imagine how strongly they wanted out of that apartment. They longed for home. How much more, in comparison, do we long for home? Do we want to go to heaven badly enough to let God be in control?

In times of grief, we question God and blame God and try to find exacting answers to our tragedies; to find answers that will give us peace. Jesus learned obedience from the things He suffered so it would be sad if we didn't learn from our trials, Hebrews 5:7-9. Life is what it is. It's life. There's going to be good and bad. But shouldn't the forgiveness that God has provided satisfy us? We are saved through Him! Redeemed!

Saved! Forgiven! All other gifts of life, all the things we enjoy are a bonus!

"Blessed be the Lord, Who daily loads us with benefits, The God of our Salvation," Psalms 68:19.

That bonus is ours! He provided for our comfort; all our sins and griefs to bear. We don't know what lies ahead. The most important thing is to know the Word. Then be the friend you would like to have and when the trials come, those friends will be by your side. Just recently I found this quote but couldn't trace the author:

When it hurts to look back and you're scared to look ahead, you can look beside you and your best friend will be there.

Not only your best earthly friend but the greatest friend of all will be there.

What a friend we have in Jesus.

Questions for study and discussion:

1. Discuss the various personalities of the apostles.

3. What are some situations that bring sadness and how should we deal with them?

Describe the faith of Stephen and lessons we can learn from it.

4. What should we do in giving and receiving help?

What is the ultimate purpose of life?

A Final Thought

An elderly man lay dying in his bed. In death's agony, he suddenly smelled the aroma of his favorite chocolate chip cookies wafting up the stairs. He gathered his remaining strength, and lifted himself from the bed. Leaning against the wall, he slowly made his way out of the bedroom, and with even greater effort forced himself down the stairs, gripping the railing with both hands.

With labored breath, he leaned against the doorframe, gazing into the kitchen. Were it not for death's agony, he would have thought himself already in heaven: There, spread out on the kitchen table were literally hundreds of his favorite chocolate chip cookies. Was it heaven? Or was it merely one final act of heroic love from his devoted wife, seeing to it that he left this world a happy man?

Mustering one great final effort, he threw himself toward the table. His aged and withered hand made its way to a cookie at the edge of the table, when his wife suddenly smacked it with a spatula.

Stay out of those, she said. *They're for the funeral.*

She's not the only person to save something for a funeral that should have been shared long before. It often seems a shame that flowers are sent to a funeral rather than beforehand when they could truly be enjoyed. Many of the comments made at funerals reflect the realization that we didn't express our feelings adequately to those we love while they were alive. *What a wonderful friend she was. I never told her how much I appreciated what she meant to me! I hope he realized how much I loved him*!

If someone is special to you, don't save it for the funeral. Share it with them now!

"Therefore comfort one another and edify one another, just as you are doing," I Thessalonians 5:11.

Editor's note: As this volume was going to print Joyce came across some more information that she felt was important enough to be included, no matter what. She shares that information below.

Two more valuable resources have come to my attention. Living a Christian life does have it's trials, but there can be more joy in your journey. Julie Adams has created a new web site that is updated weekly, entitled, "Joys of the Journey." Check out her upbeat and uplifting site at www.joysofthejourney.com <http://www.joysofthejourney.com>

Still having trouble saying just the right words? Jane McWhorter's book Special Delivery ~ Creating Paper Treasures caught my eye recently in a bookstore. It's a very complete study of encouragement through our written words, available through Publishing Designs, Inc. P.O. Box 3241 Huntsville, Al. 35810, or check your local bookstore.

Endnotes

1   <u>Tuesday's With Morrie</u> by Mitch Albom; Doubleday Publications, New York, New York, 1997.

2   <u>Men are From Mars ~ Women are from Venus,</u> by Dr. John Gray; Harper Collins Publishers, 1992.

3   <u>A Third Serving of Chicken Soup for the Soul</u> by Jack Canfield and Mark Hansen; Health Communications, Inc. Deerfield Beach, Florida, 1996.

4   <u>Christians and Cancer </u>by Mike Wilson; Xulon Press, 2006.

5   <u>Worry Free Living</u> byMinirth, Meier and Hawkins; Thomas Nelson, Publisher, 1989.

6   <u>Living with Chronic Fatigue Syndrome</u> by Timothy Kenny; Thunders Mouth Press, New York, 1994.

7   <u>The Right Way to Comfort a Friend with Cancer</u> by Jennifer Allen; Good Housekeeping Magazine; April 2006.

8   <u>On Death and Dying</u> by Elizabeth Kubler Ross; Simon and Schuster/Touchtone, 1969.

9   Roger Vaughn, Florence, Alabama.

10   <u>Songs of Hope</u> by Grace Noll Crowell; Harper and Brothers Publisher, New York, N.Y; 1938.

11   <u>The Grief Recovery Handbook</u> by John W. James and Frank Cherry, Harper Perennial, Publishers, 1988.

12   <u>Silver Boxes</u> by Florence Littauer; Thomas Nelson Publisher; 1989.

13   <u>Please Dear Friend</u> by Mary Bailey, following the death of her daughter, killed in an automobile accident on her way home from college for Thanksgiving break.

14   <u>Chicken Soup for the Grieving Soul</u> by Jack Canfield and Mark Hansen; Health Communications, Inc. Deerfield Beach, Florida, 2002.

15   <u>When God Doesn't Make Sense</u> by Dr. James Dobson, PhD. Tyndale House Publishers, 1993.

16   <u>Prayer and Providence</u>, by Homer Hailey; Religious Supply, Louisville, Kentucky, 1993.

17   <u>When Bad Things Happen to Good People</u> by Harold S. Kushner, Avon Books, New York, thought taken from page 44.

18   <u>Does God Exist?</u> by John Clayton PO Box 2704, South Bend, Indiana, 46680-2704

19   <u>On Grief and Grieving</u> by Elizabeth Kubler Ross & David Kessler; Scribner Publishers, July 2005.

20   <u>Wait</u>, by Russell Kelfer; Marianne Richmond, publisher; used with permission; www.mariannerichmond.com.

21   <u>Castaway</u>, the movie, starring Tom Hanks, written by William Broyles, Jr. December 2000.

22   <u>The Missing Piece</u> by Shel Silverstein, Harper Collins Publishers, 1976.

23   <u>A Case for Faith</u> by Lee Stroebel, Zondervan Publishing, 2000.

24   <u>A Grace Disguised</u> by Jerry Sittser; Zondervan Publishing, 1995,2004.

25   <u>The Power of Suffering</u> by John MacArthur, Victor Books, 1996.

26   <u>Plugged In: High Voltage Prayer</u> by Edwin Crozier, Streamside Supplies, 2005, page 160.

27   Reaching for the Invisible God by Philip Yancey, Zondervan Publishing, 2000; page 67.

28   Til There Was No Remedy by Bob & Sandra Waldron; Bob Waldron, Athens, Alabama.

29   www.wordpoints.com/brass- tacks/outlines/ser_0001-0050/Ser0039.html

30   Fable; source unknown.

31   101 Hymn Stories by Kenneth W. Osbeck; Kregel Publications, 1982.

32   Twelve Ordinary Men by John MacArthur; Nelson Books; 2002.

33   Forgive Me for Keeping Your Bible via House to House, Heart to Heart; Volume 12 Number 4, North Carolina Church of Christ, Killen, Al.

More Bible workbooks that you can order from Spiritbuilding.com or your favorite Christian bookstore.

Inside Out
Studying spiritual growth in bite sized pieces
Night and Day
Comparing N.T. Christianity and Islam
Church Discipline
A quarter's study on an important task for the church
Exercising Authority
How we use & understand authority on a daily basis
Compass Points
22 foundation lessons for home studies or new Christians
We're Different Because...
A workbook on authority and recent church history that ought to be taught regularly
Communing with the Lord
A study of the Lord's Supper & issues surrounding it
Marriage Through the Ages
A quarter's study of God's design for this part of our life
Parenting Through the Ages
Bible principles tested & explained by successful parents who are also a preacher, elder, grandparents and foster parents
1 & 2 Timothy and Titus
A commentary workbook on these letters from Paul
From Beneath the Altar
A workbook commentary on the book of Revelation
The Parables, Taking a Deeper Look
A relevant examination of our Lord's teaching stories
The Minor Prophets, Vol. 1 & 2, with PowerPoint CD
Old lessons that speak directly to us today
Esteemed of God, Studying the book of Daniel
Covering the man as well as the time between the testaments

Reveal In Me...
A ladies study on finding and developing one's own talents
I Will NOT Be Lukewarm, with Powerpoint CD
A ladies study on defeating mediocrity
The Gospel of John
A study for women, by a woman, on this letter of John
Sisters at War
Breaking the generation gap between sisters in Christ

Transitions - Moving Through the Twenty-Somethings with PowerPoint CD and Teacher's Manual
A relevant life study for this changing age group
Snapshots, Defining Moments in a Girl's Life
How to make godly decisions when it really matters
The Path of Peace
Relevant and important topics of study for teens
The Purity Pursuit
Helping teens achieve purity in all aspects of life
Romans, with Powerpoint CD
Putting righteousness by faith on an understandable level, for teens through adults

It's Not About Me: Becoming an A+ Teacher
A weekend seminar on how to teach the Bible to adults (and teens) and make it stick, by one of General Motors top trainers. Materials and methods are provided to teach your teachers more effective ways of communicating the important message of the Gospel. Call to discuss costs and available dates.

AUTISM, In the Eye of the Hurricane
What do you do when your child is diagnosed as autistic, the specialists are expensive, and the outlook is that nothing can be done? This is the story of one courageous couple that has set the medical community back on its heels. With faith and hard work they present a story of hope for those touched by this storm, helping their autistic son to move from permanently handicapped to the status of gifted learner.

CPSIA information can be obtained
at www.ICGtesting.com
Printed in the USA
FSHW020129050521
81117FS

9 780977 475452